What's What™
in
SPORTS

What's What™
in
SPORTS

The Visual Glossary of the Sports World

Reginald Bragonier Jr.
and
David Fisher

HAMMOND®
INCORPORATED
MAPLEWOOD, NEW JERSEY 07040-1396

Printed in the United States of America

Library of Congress Cataloging in Publication Data

Fisher, David, 1946-
  What's what in sports.

  Includes index.
  1. Sports—Dictionaries.   I. Bragonier, Reginald.
II. Title.
GV567.F58   1984   796′.03   84-9032
ISBN 8-8437-3528-7 hardcover
ISBN 0-8437-3529-5 softcover

WHO'S WHO IN WHAT'S WHAT ™

EDITORS
Reginald Bragonier Jr., David Fisher

MANAGING EDITOR
Sandra Roemer Dorfman

SENIOR RESEARCH EDITOR
Glenn Deutsch

ASSOCIATE RESEARCH EDITORS
Stephanie Bernardo, Deborah Friedman, Robert Henry,
Dana Keeler, Marion Ratner, Shane Mitchell

DESIGN & PRODUCTION
Barnett Design Group

PROJECT MANAGER
Dennis Peter Barnett

DESIGN DIRECTOR
David Barnett

DESIGNER
Donna Moll

ASSOCIATE DESIGNERS
Jan Cain, Derek Fox, Patrick Weisel

ILLUSTRATOR
Claire Seiffert

NAUTICAL ILLUSTRATOR
Steven Davis

CONTRIBUTING PHOTOGRAPHERS
Nancie Battaglia, Steve Borowski, Rich Clarkson,
Joe DiMaggio/JoAnne Kalish, Guy Gurney,
Walter Iooss, Al Messerschmidt, Brent Nicastro,
Eduardo Patino, Phillip Stark, Strobe Studio

SEQUENTIAL PHOTOGRAPHY
Globus Brothers Studio

MOTION PHOTOGRAPHY
Ben Rose and Globus Brothers Studio

TYPOGRAPHY
Expertype, Inc.

TABLE OF CONTENTS

*Olympic Sport

FOREWORD

WHAT IT IS

WHAT'S WHAT™ IN SPORTS presents the world of competitive athletics in a way that has never been attempted before. It is a book that celebrates the beauty and grace of sport, while also serving as the first visual reference book for this special world. Through the use of photography and detailed illustration, it tells—and shows—the reader the object of most major sports, how games are played, and what equipment is used. It also identifies parts of playing fields, courts and arenas, as well as illustrating essential moves, maneuvers and plays.

WHAT'S WHAT™ IN SPORTS is not intended to be a substitute for engaging in or witnessing sports events. Rather, it is a valuable adjunct to the sports world, enabling anyone to better understand what happens, what to look for and how to score or judge contests. It prepares viewers beforehand for what will take place and afterwards helps them appreciate what has happened. When a gymnast performs a perfect maneuver, a "10," for example, it happens so quickly that it is virtually impossible to understand what was attempted and how well the feat was executed. WHAT'S WHAT™ IN SPORTS will bridge that gap, and in the process enhance the reader's appreciation for the glorious moments in sports.

HOW IT WORKS

We have extracted from each sport the elements and information that are essential for an understanding of how it is played. In team sports and sports whose outcome is determined by strictly defined scoring rules, this information includes the playing field, its dimensions, the positioning of players, and examples of team movements. In sports whose outcome is determined by a judging system, we have illustrated the basic movements that must be performed and the general criteria by which they will be judged, usually shown sequentially.

A typical page begins with a textblock that provides overall information about the sport or event, as well as additional background information. Lines running directly to illustrations clearly identify objects and their individual parts. Dotted lines are used to indicate pieces of equipment which are not readily visible. Brackets have been used to indicate areas.

To locate any sport, begin with the table of contents which lists all sports alphabetically. Individual events, which comprise the sport, are listed under the general heading. Pole vaulting, for example, is listed under Track and Field. The comprehensive index lists every sport, event, piece of equipment and playing field alphabetically.

AND WHY

This book's predecessor, *WHAT'S WHAT™: A Visual Glossary of the Physical World*, has been hailed by critics as either the most entertaining reference book or the most informative general book published in decades.

We have tried to bring the same combination of entertainment and information to this book by carefully selecting photographs and illustrations that will enable the reader to not only understand how a sport is played but also how to better appreciate the fine points.

We have been aided in our task by many well-known players and coaches, as well as experts in various fields of graphic endeavor. Use of this book, it is hoped, will enable every reader to gain a fuller understanding of the skill and effort that goes into every sport, and to come away informed and entertained.

In championship aerobatics, teams of pilots compete by performing spectacular flying feats and maneuvers in three programs: a known compulsory program, composed of figures in both normal and inverted flight (seven minutes); an unknown compulsory program, consisting of at least 15 figures chosen the day before by heads of delegations (seven minutes); and a free program, in which contestants may fly up to 30 figures of their own choosing in nine minutes.

Contestants must fly within an *aerobatic box*, a zone of 880 by 1,100 yards which is clearly marked on the ground. Additionally, they may fly no higher than 1,100 yards or lower than 110, or they risk being penalized.

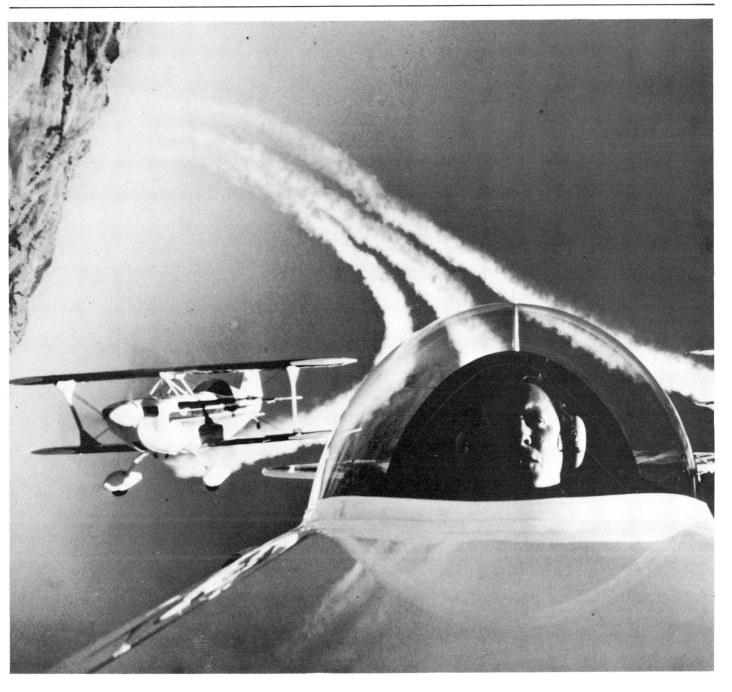

Men and women's teams of at least three and not more than five pilots each compete in 150- to 350-hp piston-engined aircraft. They are judged for each figure performed and given between zero and 10 points. To arrive at the final score, the two highest and lowest scores are eliminated. The remaining scores are averaged and multiplied by each figure's *difficulty coefficient*, between one and 35. The pilot or team with the highest number of points in all programs wins.

Aerobatic maneuvers number in the thousands. Most, however, are composed of combinations of *rolls, loops, spins, climbs* and *dives.*

In addition to the figures shown below, *fliers* may perform the following maneuvers: *Wingover,* a

BIPLANE: NORMAL FLIGHT (TOP),
INVERTED FLIGHT/NEGATIVE FLIGHT (BOTTOM)

ELEVATOR · HORIZONTAL STABILIZER · RUDDER · VERTICAL STABILIZER · AILERON · CANOPY · UPPER WING · PROPELLER · SPINNER · ENGINE COWLING · LANDING GEAR STRUT · REGISTRATION NUMBER · AILERON SLAVE TUBE · INTERPLANE STRUT · LOWER WING · WHEEL/TIRE · WHEEL PANTS

BASIC COMPETITIVE FIGURES & MANEUVERS

VERTICAL HALF ROLL

VERTICAL EIGHT

SPIN

reversing maneuver in which the aircraft changes heading by 180 degrees; *Chandelle*, a coordinated turn-reversing maneuver during which the maximum amount of altitude is gained; *Immelmann*, a half loop immediately followed by a half roll; *Cuban Eight*, a combination of partial loops, 45-degree dives and half rolls; *Avalanche*, a snap roll on top of a loop; and *Humpty Bumps*, a family of maneuvers characterized by a vertical line with climbing half rolls, a half loop over to a diving vertical line, followed by recovery to horizontal flight at the same altitude as the entry.

ROLLING CIRCLE WITH FOUR HORIZONTAL ROLLS

TAIL SIDE/WHIP STALL

BARREL ROLL

HORIZONTAL EIGHT/LAYOUT EIGHT

HORIZONTAL SLOW ROLL

STALL TURN/HAMMERHEAD

In *closed course air racing*, aircraft in five classes, from homebuilt planes powered by 60-hp engines to modified World War II fighters with 3,000-hp engines, race over fixed distances marked by turning pylons.

In International Formula One, the most popular class, aircraft approximately 16 feet long, with a similar *wingspan*, reach speeds of 240-mph powered by 100-hp engines.

In *air starts*, racers, already airborne, form up on a *pace plane* that dives across the starting line and pulls away. In *racehorse starts*, aircraft line up on the runway and start when a flag is dropped.

Handicap races, for stock aircraft, are flown cross country.

COCKPIT

CYLINDER HEAD TEMPERATURE GAUGE
'G' METER
OIL TEMPERATURE GAUGE
OIL PRESSURE GAUGE
THROTTLE
ALTIMETER
CARBURETOR HEAT CONTROL
MAGNETO SWITCH
ALTIMETER SETTING KNOB
AIRSPEED INDICATOR
TACHOMETER
CYLINDER HEAD TEMPERATURE SELECT KNOB
FUEL TANK SIGHT GAUGE
FLAP HANDLE
PITCH & TRIM ADJUSTMENT
CONTROL STICK

FORMULA ONE RACECOURSE

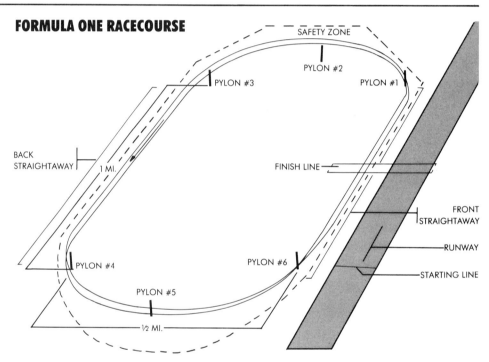

SAFETY ZONE
PYLON #3
PYLON #2
PYLON #1
BACK STRAIGHTAWAY
1 MI.
FINISH LINE
FRONT STRAIGHTAWAY
RUNWAY
PYLON #4
PYLON #6
STARTING LINE
PYLON #5
½ MI.

FORMULA ONE AIRCRAFT

DECAL
ACCESS DOOR
RACE NUMBER
REGISTRATION NUMBER
FUSELAGE
ENGINE COWLING
RUNWAY MARKINGS

The ascent of a hot air balloon, or *montgolfier*, is controlled by regulating the temperature of the air inside the nylon envelope and by the amount of *ballast*, usually water or sandbags, carried in the gondola. At higher altitudes cooler air slows a balloon's ascent. Its lateral movement is determined by wind speed and direction. A *drag rope*, or *trail rope*, hangs from the wicker basket to provide stability in flight and to slow the balloon down on landing.

A *rip panel* near the top, or *apex*, of the envelope is opened to deflate the balloon.

Ballooners compete for flight duration, navigational skills and altitude achieved.

BASKET/GONDOLA

TETHER BLOCK
STANDARD BLAST VALVE
FUEL HOSES

BURNER ASSEMBLY

SIDE RAIL COVER

PYROMETER
PADDING
OWNER'S PLAQUE
WINDOW
CARRYING HANDLE

ON-OFF SWITCH
ALTIMETER
CHAMPAGNE BOTTLE
REMOTE ELECTRONIC BLAST VALVE CONTROLS
QUANTITY GAUGE
FUEL LINE
FUEL TANK STRAPS
HANDLE

REGISTRATION NUMBER/"N" NUMBER
LOAD CORDS
PANELS
PANEL SEAMS
SKIRT
PRESSURE SKIRT
ENVELOPE/BAG
BASKET/GONDOLA

FUEL TANK
SCUFF PAD
HARDWOOD BASE

ELECTRONIC IGNITION CHASSIS BOX
BURNER
PRESSURE GAUGE

HOT AIR BALLOON

FREE FLIGHT SKIRT

FAN ASSEMBLY
QUICK RELEASE CLAMPS

BURNER ASSEMBLY

TETHER BLOCK
PRESSURE FAN ASSEMBLY
PADDED FAN
MOTOR GUARD

Gliders are either towed to a suitable height by an airplane, called a *tug*, or launched from the ground by auto towing or winch towing. Like *sailplanes*, which engage in *soaring* and are piloted by *sailplaners*, gliders gain altitude and remain aloft by riding rising currents of warm air, or *thermals*. Competitors are judged on altitude gained, distance covered and speed on a closed course.

In hang gliding, also known as *self soaring* and *sky surfing*, contestants compete in *self launch open class*, in which the pilot must carry his craft to the *launch site* and *foot launch* it himself, and *open class*, in which any hang glider may be used and launched with the assistance of one person.

HANG GLIDER

LEADING EDGE — KING POST — NOSE PLATE — BATTENS — SAIL — HELMET — RIGGING — FLIGHT INSTRUMENTS — PARACHUTE — COCOON HARNESS — CB RADIO — CONTROL BAR

GLIDER COCKPIT

ELECTRICAL SWITCH FOR VARIOMETER — VARIOMETER — TURN AND SLIP INDICATOR — AIR SPEED INDICATOR — 'G' METER — COMPASS — VERTICAL SPEED INDICATOR — ALTIMETER — ALTIMETER SETTING KNOB — TOW RELEASE KNOB — CONTROL STICK — STATIC PORT TUBE — TOW HOOK RELEASE SPRING — RUDDER CABLE — FLAP CONTROL KNOB — FLAP CONTROL MECHANISM

GLIDER

AILERON — HORIZONTAL STABILIZER — ELEVATOR — RUDDER — VERTICAL STABILIZER — COCKPIT CANOPY — PITOT TUBE — AILERON

There are three events in competitive sky diving. In style competition, *sky divers* perform stunts, such as spirals and loops, during *free fall*, the period between jumping from the airplane and opening their chutes. In accuracy competition, divers are judged on how close they land to a small disk in the target area. In *relative work*, four-, eight- and 10- man teams pass a baton to one another or attempt hook ups in order to form different patterns.

All competitive *sport parachuting* is conducted over a hazard-free *dropping zone*, or *DZ*. The ground surrounding it is called the *overshoot area*.

Jumpmasters are in charge of all jumps from aircraft.

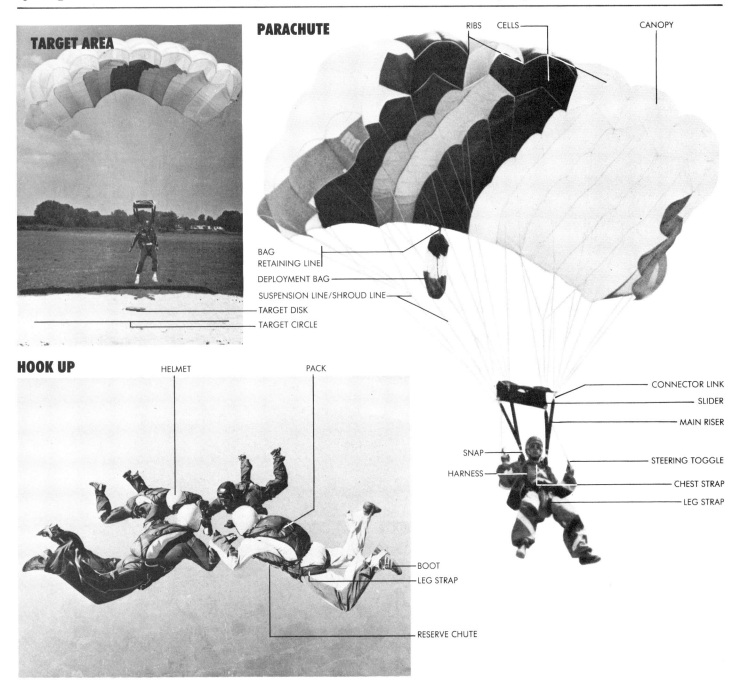

TARGET AREA

BAG RETAINING LINE
DEPLOYMENT BAG
SUSPENSION LINE/SHROUD LINE
TARGET DISK
TARGET CIRCLE

PARACHUTE

RIBS   CELLS   CANOPY

CONNECTOR LINK
SLIDER
MAIN RISER
SNAP
STEERING TOGGLE
HARNESS
CHEST STRAP
LEG STRAP

HOOK UP

HELMET   PACK

BOOT
LEG STRAP

RESERVE CHUTE

Anyone who fishes for sport is called an *angler, fisherman, sport-fisherman,* or *Izaak Walton.* He or she uses *freshwater* or *saltwater tackle* and *live* or *artificial bait,* depending on the fish's *feeding pattern* or habits.

When a fish *takes the bait,* or lure, the fisherman puts tension on the line to *set the hook* and drive the barb home, called *striking the fish,* and plays it until it is *landed, taken, boated,* or *tagged* and *released.*

Fishing tournaments and *world record catches* are governed by specific limitations on tackle.

The fish on page 9, *piscatoris bassasailus,* is a whimsical combination of a freshwater and saltwater *game fish.*

BASIC FISHING RIG

- ROD/POLE
- LINE
- BOBBER/FLOAT
- CLIP/PIN/LOOP
- SINKER/WEIGHT/SPLIT SHOT
- HOOK
- BAIT

FISH

- DORSAL FIN/SPINY DORSAL FIN
- SPINY RAYS
- CAUDAL KEELS
- TAIL FIN/ CAUDAL FIN
- GILL OPENING
- GILL COVER/OPERCULUM/OPERCULE PREOPERCLE
- NOSTRIL
- EYE
- UPPER JAW
- SNOUT
- BILL
- MOUTH
- MAXILLA
- LOWER JAW/MANDIBLE
- HEAD
- PECTORAL FIN
- CAUDAL PEDUNCLE
- TAIL
- ANAL FIN
- SCALES
- TRUNK
- VENTER/BELLY
- PELVIC FINS/VENTRAL FINS

LIVE BAIT CAGE

- WIRE EYE BOLT
- SCREEN TUBE
- ROTATING BAIT LID
- END COVERS
- SHOULDER CARRYING CORD

HOOK/FISHHOOK

- GAP
- BARB
- POINT
- EYE
- SHANK
- BEND
- LEADER
- SWIVEL
- THROAT

TACKLE BOX

- MOTION SICKNESS PILLS
- DRYING RIB
- TOOLS
- FISHING LINE
- LEADERS
- LURES
- HOOKS/FISHHOOKS
- SPOONS
- DEEP-DIVING PLUG/ CRANK BAIT
- TACKLE/GEAR/FISHING EQUIPMENT

Artificial flies are tiny hooks, dressed with hair, yarn, feathers fur, or other material meant to suggest insects, small swimmers or crustaceans on which fish feed.

The fly is attached to a tippet, a short section of fine line at the end of a tapered leader.

Flies may be used in different ways, depending on their design and the bait they are meant to imitate. Dry flies are worked on the surface. Streamers, *nymphs* and *bucktails* are used at various depths.

A rod's *'action'* is its degree of bend, dependent on its *taper*, and the manner in which it affects casting and playing a fish.

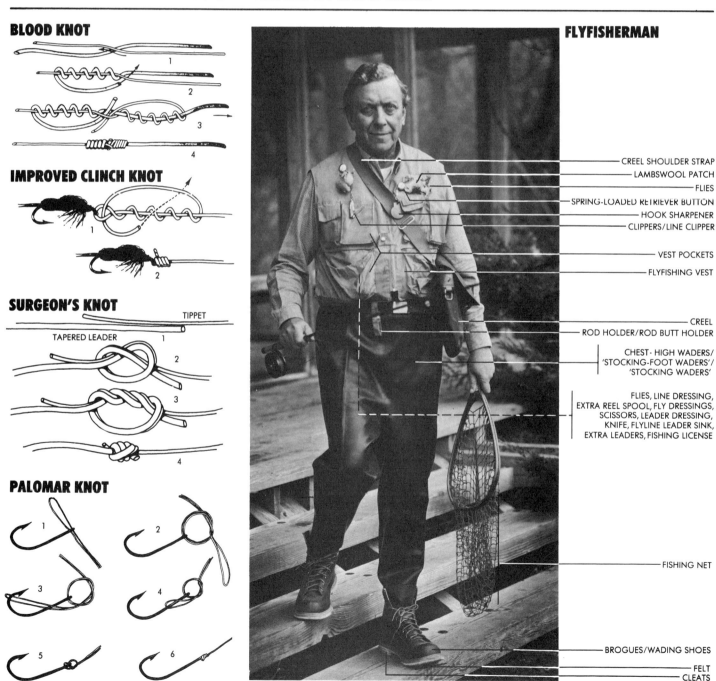

BLOOD KNOT

1

2

3

4

IMPROVED CLINCH KNOT

1

2

SURGEON'S KNOT

TIPPET

TAPERED LEADER

1

2

3

4

PALOMAR KNOT

1

2

3

4

5

6

FLYFISHERMAN

CREEL SHOULDER STRAP
LAMBSWOOL PATCH
FLIES
SPRING-LOADED RETRIEVER BUTTON
HOOK SHARPENER
CLIPPERS/LINE CLIPPER

VEST POCKETS
FLYFISHING VEST

CREEL
ROD HOLDER/ROD BUTT HOLDER

CHEST- HIGH WADERS/
'STOCKING-FOOT WADERS'/
'STOCKING WADERS'

FLIES, LINE DRESSING,
EXTRA REEL SPOOL, FLY DRESSINGS,
SCISSORS, LEADER DRESSING,
KNIFE, FLYLINE LEADER SINK,
EXTRA LEADERS, FISHING LICENSE

FISHING NET

BROGUES/WADING SHOES
FELT
CLEATS

FLY ROD

FERRULE
TIP
TIP-TOP

FERRULE
SNAKE GUIDE
MIDDLE/JOINT

KEEPER RING
BUTT
RING GUIDE/
BUTT GUIDE

WINDING CHECK
HAND GRIP
SCREW-LOCKING
NUT AND HOOD
REEL SEAT

REEL-SEAT WASHER
REAR HOOD AND BUTT CAP

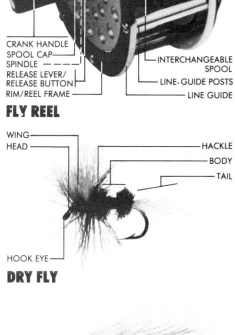

TAIL PLATE/BACK SIDEPLATE
REEL FOOT

DRAG SYSTEM &
ANTI-REVERSE
SPOOL LOCK

REEL-FOOT POSTS
HEAD PLATE/
FRONT SIDEPLATE

DRAG/DRAG CONTROL
KNOB/DRAG HUB

CRANK HANDLE
SPOOL CAP
SPINDLE
RELEASE LEVER/
RELEASE BUTTON
RIM/REEL FRAME

INTERCHANGEABLE
SPOOL
LINE-GUIDE POSTS
LINE GUIDE

FLY REEL

WING
HEAD

HACKLE
BODY
TAIL

HOOK EYE

DRY FLY

TINSEL BODY/TAG

WET FLY/STREAMER

FLYCASTING TECHNIQUE

REACH
1
PULL
2
LIFT
3
4
STOP 5
REACH
6
7
PULL

CAST
8

9

SHOOT
10

In spin casting or *bait casting*, the weight of the lure or bait uncoils the line from the spool.

Fishermen using *open-faced spinning reels* control the length of the cast with their index finger, *feathering* the unrolling line to pre-vent overshooting the target.

In bait casting, the reel's spool is not stationary. It revolves and can therefore overrun, or *backlash*. Since a plug is the most common lure used in bait casting, the technique is often called '*plug casting.*'

Spinners rotate and vibrate when drawn through the water. *Spoons* wobble and flash. Plugs and jigs imitate live bait when cast and *retrieved*.

SPINNING TRAVEL SET

POCKET
PADDED CASE
ROD/PACK ROD
SPINNING REEL

REEL

FOOT/ROD MOUNT
HANDLE
LEG/STEM
TRIP/DOG
CRANK
BAIL/PICKUP ARM
SKIRT
ANTI-REVERSE LEVER/ ANTI-REVERSE LOCK
SPOOL
DRAG-ADJUSTMENT KNOB/ DRAG KNOB/DRAG BRAKE/ BRAKE SCREW
REAR BEARING
CUP/FLYER
GEAR HOUSING COVER PLATE
FLANGE
LINE ROLLER/LINE GUIDE
BEARING COVER
SILENT ANTI-REVERSE HOUSING

PENN 150SS

ROD

LOCK RING
HANDLE/ BUTT GRIP
HOOD/ SEAT RING
REEL SEAT
FOREGRIP/FORWARD GRIP
CHUCK
BUTT GUIDE
FEMALE FERRULE
MALE FERRULE
WINDING/WIND
GUIDE
TOP RING/END RING
TIP-TOP
BUTT CAP
BUTT SECTION
MID-SECTION SHAFT
ROD TIP/BLADE

LURES   PLUG

EYE
BODY
LIP/BILL
TREBLE HOOK
HOOK HANGER

JIG

HEAD
SKIRT
HOOK
EYE

SPINNER

BLADE DECAL
BLADE
CLEVIS
EYE
OVAL BEAD
BELL BEAD
SPACER BEAD
WEIGHT
HOOK
TAIL/SKIRT
WIRE SHAFT

OVERHEAD SPINNING CAST

1. AIM   2. STOP   3. CAST   4. RELEASE

Trolling consists of pulling baits or lures behind a boat. *Surface trolling* and *deep* or *bottom trolling* require different methods.

In deep trolling, for example, *lead-core* or *wire line* is used. In *depth-control fishing* where a down-rigger is used, a heavy weight is attached to wire line wound on a large wheel. The lure and leader are fastened by a *breakaway coupling* to the weight and lowered to the desired depth, measured by turns on the downrigger wheel or a meter.

Vessels used for trolling may be large and motorized or small and manually operated. Quiet electric trolling motors are favored by anglers stalking fish they don't want to 'spook' or scare away.

BASS BOAT/BASS RIG

- BOW-MOUNTED DEPTH SOUNDER
- ELECTRIC TROLLING MOTOR
- CASTING DECKS/ CASTING PLATFORMS
- BOW CONTROL PANEL
- HANDRAIL
- CONSOLE
- IN-DASH DEPTH SOUNDER
- LIVE (BAIT) WELL
- ICE CHEST/STORAGE COMPARTMENT
- OUTBOARD ENGINE

DEEP TROLLING RIGS

- 25'–125'
- 25'–125'
- IN-LINE SINKER
- 26'
- SURGICAL TUBING
- 3-WAY SWIVEL
- BELL SINKER
- 25'
- BUCKTAIL LURE

DOWNRIGGER

- BOOM
- SWIVEL HEAD ASSEMBLY & SIDEPLATE
- SWIVEL-HEAD PULLEY WHEEL
- BODY
- CUSHION SWIVEL KIT
- ROD HOLDER
- DEPTH METER READING
- DOG & RATCHET SHAFT ASSEMBLY
- DEPTH METER ASSEMBLY
- CABLE WHEEL ASSEMBLY
- CRANK ASSEMBLY
- CLAMP
- CLUTCH SHAFT & BEARING
- CRANK HANDLE
- PLATE
- BASE LOCKING
- BASE

UMBRELLA RIG

- HOOK
- TUBE LURE
- LEADER

TROLLING REEL

- HANDLE
- STAR DRAG
- COUNTERBALANCE
- LOCKING NUT
- ANTI-REVERSE LEVER
- SIDEPLATE ASSEMBLY/ REEL HOUSING
- REEL FOOT
- PLASTIC SPOOL
- MANUFACTURER PLATE/SPEC PLATE
- SPOOL CENTERING & TENSION KNOB
- SIDEPLATE

In surf fishing, oversized gear and a two-handed technique are generally required to reach fish in the *striking zone*.

Surfcasters may offer bait to 'bottom feeders' and game fish alike with a double-level fishfinder rig, or use only lures that imitate *bait fish* if they are interested in game fish alone.

Anglers who *bottom fish* use *dead*, *cut*, or *strip bait*, or live bait. Their *terminal tackle*, the equipment at the end of the line, is held fast on the bottom by heavy sinkers.

Surfcasters may *net* or *gaff* fish as they near shore, or they may *beach* their catch by dragging it out of the water and up the beach.

SURFCASTING TECHNIQUE

DOUBLE-LEVEL FISHFINDER RIG

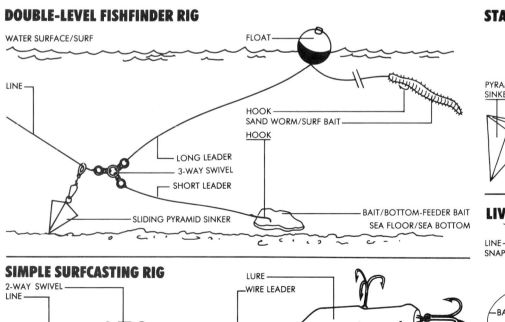

WATER SURFACE/SURF

FLOAT

LINE

HOOK
SAND WORM/SURF BAIT

HOOK

LONG LEADER
3-WAY SWIVEL
SHORT LEADER

SLIDING PYRAMID SINKER

BAIT/BOTTOM-FEEDER BAIT
SEA FLOOR/SEA BOTTOM

STANDARD BOTTOM FISHING RIG

3-WAY SWIVEL

PYRAMID SINKER

HOOK

LIVE MINNOW RIG

LINE
SNAP

2-WAY SWIVEL
SINKER LEADER
SINKER

HOOK
BAIT LEADER

BAITFISH/MINNOW

SIMPLE SURFCASTING RIG

2-WAY SWIVEL
LINE

LURE
WIRE LEADER

Anglers troll for *big game fish* with oversized lures or baits. When a fish 'feeds' the angler strikes it to set the hook, then reduces the drag on the reel as the fish makes its first *run*.

The main purpose of the fighting chair is to allow the angler to use his or her back and leg muscles against the fish.

With the rod butt resting in the chair's gimballed socket, the angler then begins pumping the rod between vertical and horizontal, taking in *slack line* on each drop.

When the fish is alongside and the *mate* has the angler's leader in hand, the fish is said to be *brought to wire*. Prior to *boating*, a fish's tail is immobilized with a gaff or *flying gaff*.

USING THE FIGHTING CHAIR

1. QUICK DROP

2. PUMP

3. REDUCE DRAG AND WAIT

FIGHTING CHAIR HARNESS

ROPE CONNECTOR/REEL CONNECTOR
BUCKET HARNESS/SEA HARNESS

GROMMETS
SAFETY SNAP
NYLON WEBBING/
ANTI-ROPE CHAFE STRIP
O-RING

FIGHTING CHAIR

ADJUSTABLE BACK REST/
STEERING HANDLE

SEAT

SEATBACK

CHAIR LOCKING HANDLE
ROUNDED SEAT FRONT
STRIKING ARMS

ARM
ARM CUSHION

SIDE GIMBAL/
GIMBALLED SOCKET
FRONT GIMBAL
FOOT REST LEGS

FRONT GIMBAL
BRACKET
ADJUSTABLE
LEG BRACKETS

ADJUSTABLE FOOT REST
DECK PLATE/DECK MOUNT
DOUBLE BALL-BEARING STANCHION

BIG GAME ROD

BUTT
GIMBAL

REEL SEAT

GRIP

ROD-WINDING THREAD
BLANK
ROLLER

GUIDE
ROLLER TIP

BIG GAME REEL

REEL REINFORCEMENT
ANTI-REVERSE LEVER
HANDLE
SIDEPLATE /
SIDEPLATE ASSEMBLY/REEL HOUSING
FIGHTING BELT/BRACKETS

STAR DRAG

MANUFACTURER PLATE/SPEC PLATE
STAINLESS STEEL SPOOL
REEL FOOT
SPOOL CENTERING & TENSION KNOB

In *target archery*, archers shoot *rounds*, or a specific number of arrows from various fixed distances. After shooting three arrows within 2½ minutes, which constitutes an *end*, archers total their points and are replaced at the shooting line by the next competitor. Each arrow landing in the target, or leaving a mark discernible by the *scorer*, is worth the value of the scoring zone in which it struck. The archer with the most points wins.

Target archery competitions may consist of numerous rounds and last as many as four days.

Field archers move about a forest-like terrain shooting at animal-shaped targets.

The *upshot* is the final arrow shot in a competition.

ARCHER/BOWMAN IN HOLD POSITION

TARGET

NOCK
LIMB TIP
BOWSTRING
UPPER LIMB
FACE SIDE
BACK/BELLY SIDE
STABILIZER ROD
COMPENSATOR
TARGET ARROW
HANDLE RISER
BOW SIGHT
FINGER SLING
ARROWHEAD/POINT/PILE/HEAD
ARROW REST
KISSER
ANCHOR POINT
DRAWING HAND
ARM GUARD/ BRACER
BOW ARM
VARIWEIGHT
QUIVER BELT
QUIVER
LOWER LIMB
RECURVE

SCORING ZONES POINT VALUE:
BULL'S EYE/GOLD/10
9
8
7
6
5
4
3
2
1
BALE/BUTT/MATT/BOSS
PETTICOAT
GROUP
PIN HOLE
STAND
TARGET FACE – 31½" OR 48" DIA.

MEN'S ARCHERY FIELD

WOMEN'S ARCHERY FIELD

SAFETY ZONE
TARGETS
77 YDS.
66 YDS.
55 YDS.
33 YDS.
99 YDS.
77 YDS.
55 YDS.
33 YDS.
SHOOTING LINES
WAITING LINE
16'3"

ARROW

CREST/CRESTING
SHAFT
COCK FEATHER
HEN FEATHERS
NOCK
FLETCHING/VANES/FEATHERS

Indianapolis-type and *Formula* cars are *open-wheel, single-seat, open-cockpit racing cars*, differing mostly in weight and engine size. *'Indy cars'* race on a banked, oval *speedway* where *drivers 'put down rubber'* to stay in the *'groove,'* but sometimes fall *'in the marbles,'* the *slick* part of the track. In *closed-circuit road racing*, Formula drivers take *Esses*, continuous left-right turns, and *chicanes*, turns formed by temporary barriers. A *pace car* leads the *starting field* to a *safe start*. A race lasts a certain number of *miles, laps* or *hours*. During the race a *green* flag indicates go, *yellow* means caution, *red* means stop racing and a black-and-white *checkered* flag is waved at the finish line.

INDY CAR

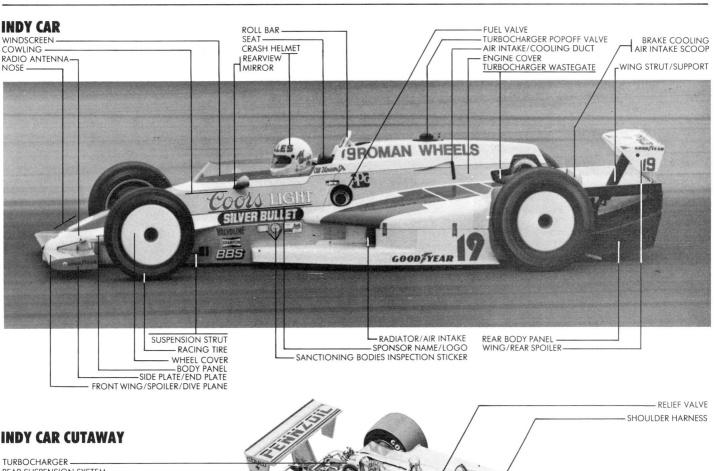

WINDSCREEN
COWLING
RADIO ANTENNA
NOSE

ROLL BAR
SEAT
CRASH HELMET
REARVIEW
MIRROR

FUEL VALVE
TURBOCHARGER POPOFF VALVE
AIR INTAKE/COOLING DUCT
ENGINE COVER
TURBOCHARGER WASTEGATE

BRAKE COOLING
AIR INTAKE SCOOP
WING STRUT/SUPPORT

SUSPENSION STRUT
RACING TIRE
WHEEL COVER
BODY PANEL
SIDE PLATE/END PLATE
FRONT WING/SPOILER/DIVE PLANE

RADIATOR/AIR INTAKE
SPONSOR NAME/LOGO
SANCTIONING BODIES INSPECTION STICKER

REAR BODY PANEL
WING/REAR SPOILER

INDY CAR CUTAWAY

RELIEF VALVE
SHOULDER HARNESS

TURBOCHARGER
REAR SUSPENSION SYSTEM

POPOFF VALVE
ENGINE
CYLINDER HEADS
FUSELAGE
FUEL INTAKE VALVE
EXHAUST SYSTEM

SIDEPOD

OIL COOLER

DISC BRAKE
RACK & PINION STEERING AND SUSPENSION SYSTEMS
FORWARD BULKHEAD
BRAKE FLUID RESERVOIR

TRACK

OUTSIDE RETAINING WALL
REMOTE CAMERAS
FLAGMAN
OFFICIAL'S OBSERVATION DECK
GRANDSTANDS
PRESS BOX
UPPER DECK

PITBOARD AREA
WINDSOCK
WINDSOCK POLE
SCORING PYLON
AMBULANCE
FIRE TRUCK

CONTROL TOWER
CAMERA POSITION
LEAD CARS
SCORING LIGHTS

SAFE POINT WIRE FENCE
'IN THE MARBLES'
WHEEL FENCE
RACING TRACK/SURFACE
THE FIELD/RACE CARS

INSIDE TRACK RETAINING WALL
DIVIDER LINE
PIT RUNWAY
PITS
PIT LINE

PACE CAR
SAFETY LINE
PAVED SHOULDER/APRON
ESCAPE ROAD

PIT CREW

FIRE CREWMAN
FUEL OVERFLOW MAN
PIT STEWARD/SANCTIONING-BODY OFFICIAL
PIT HEADSET
FUEL HOSE
REFUELER

FULLFACE HELMET
RIGHT SIDE TIRECHANGER/WHEELCHANGER
FIREPROOF GLOVES
QUICK-DISCONNECT REFUELING SAFETY VALVE

AIR CHUCK

LEFT SIDE TIRECHANGER/WHEELCHANGER

JACKING AIR HOSE
FIRE EXTINGUISHER
FIREPROOF UNIFORM
FUEL OVERFLOW HOSE

MANIFOLD PRESSURE GAUGE

COCKPIT FIRE EXTINGUISHER ACTIVATOR BUTTON

FIRE EXTINGUISHER ON-OFF SWITCH
TACHOMETER

STEERING WHEEL

WATER TEMPERATURE GAUGE

HAND STOP
OIL PRESSURE GAUGE
DUMMY BUTTON

ELECTRICAL SYSTEM KILL SWITCH

STEERING HUB/WHEEL HUB

RADIO PUSH-TO-TALK SWITCH
RADIO WIRING

DRIVER'S COMPARTMENT/COCKPIT/INSTRUMENT PANEL/DASH

Each drag racing *event, acceleration contest*, or *run*, involves two-car *heats*, the winner of which is deemed the *eliminator*. Vehicles include *slingshot dragsters* and *funny cars* whose mismatched *hulls* and *chassis* give them an unusual appearance. The *Christmas tree* is situated in the middle of a divided, two-lane *straight-line course, drag strip*, or *dragway. Elapsed time, 'ET*,' is computed from the moment a car breaks a *light beam* at the *starting line* until it breaks a similar beam at the *finish*. Most drivers try to leave between the flashes of the fifth amber *starting light* and green *GO-light*. A car leaving prematurely makes a *foul start*, and is said to be *red-lighting*.

HELMET
EYEPORT SHIELD
VENT PORT
NOSE SHROUD & BREATHING FILTER
NECK SOCK
HELMET SKIRT
SHOULDER HARNESS
DRIVING GLOVE
DRIVING SUIT
LAP BELT
ANTI-SUBMARINE BELT/CROTCH STRAP
RACING SHOE

DRIVER'S FIRE SUIT

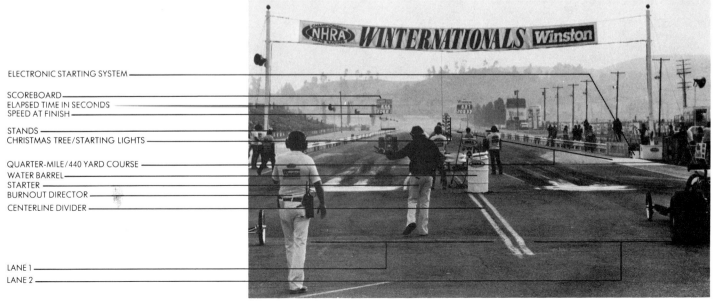

ELECTRONIC STARTING SYSTEM
SCOREBOARD
ELAPSED TIME IN SECONDS
SPEED AT FINISH
STANDS
CHRISTMAS TREE/STARTING LIGHTS
QUARTER-MILE/440 YARD COURSE
WATER BARREL
STARTER
BURNOUT DIRECTOR
CENTERLINE DIVIDER
LANE 1
LANE 2

TRACK/DRAG STRIP/DRAGWAY

MAIN WING/AIR FOIL
WING STRUT/SUPPORT BAR
AIR SCOOP/INTAKE VALVES
ROLL CAGE
ALUMINUM RIM
FRONT SPOILER
FRONT WHEEL
BODY
ENGINE
INJECTOR
SUPERCHARGER
VALVE COVER & HEAD/
EXHAUST HEADER

PRE-STAGE

STAGE

AMBER/YELLOW
PRE-STARTING LIGHTS

AMBER/YELLOW
SEQUENCED
STARTING LIGHTS

POWER CORD

GREEN GO-LIGHT

RED FOUL-LIGHT

POLE

BASE

CHRISTMAS TREE/STARTING LIGHTS

WATER VENTS

PARACHUTE PACK

RACING SLICK/TIRE
ZOOMIES / HEADERS
DRIVER
FIRE EXTINGUISHER
FUEL TANK

TOW PIN

SPINDLE

FRONT AXLE/SUSPENSION

Sports cars are comprised of many different types of race cars. They compete in a *Group* or *Class* determined by performance, design or engine size, (including *Sedan, Production, Grand Touring (GT)* and single-seat *Formulas*) on both open road and twisting track courses. In endurance events known as *factory* or *team challenges*, two to five drivers alternate in one car.

Stock cars are modified factory production vehicles. Their interiors have been stripped and safety rollcages have been installed. *Heavy-duty suspensions* are adjusted for the way dirt or asphalt track corners are inclined, or *banked*. Short, oval tracks are called '*bullpens*.' The first car to cover the race distance wins.

SPORTS CAR

CATCH FENCING

CONCRETE RETAINING WALL

FOOTING

STALL GATE
ADJUSTABLE SECONDARY WING PART
SIDE PLATE
ADJUSTABLE PRIMARY WING PART
ADJUSTABLE REAR WING/SPOILER/TAIL
FLOW ROOF OVERLAY
PRODUCTION ROOF
REAR DECK OVERLAY
ROLLCAGE
OIL FILLER
SIDE SKIRT/AEROFOIL
SIDE MIRROR
FUEL FILLER
HOOD PIN
BRAKE COOLING DUCT
HEADLIGHT BOX
OIL COOLER
SPLITTER

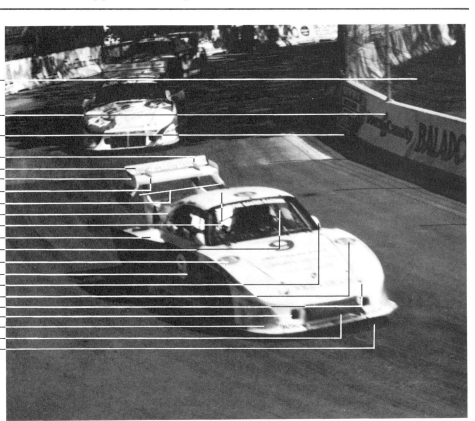

STOCK CAR

ANTENNA

REAR SPOILER
GLASSLESS WINDOW
DRIVER'S SAFETY NET

ROLLCAGE

HOOD PINS
FIREWALL

SCREEN-WIRE COVER

JACK-POINT INDICATOR

FRONT SPOILER

Badminton is usually played indoors by individuals or two-player teams. The object is to hit the 'bird' over the net, in bounds, so the opposition cannot return it. The serving team continues to serve until losing a *rally* or committing a *fault*, a rules violation such as serving overhand, touching the net, moving before the server strikes the bird, or not serving diagonally across court. Points may only be scored by the serving team. In doubles, both players serve each *inning*, or change of serve.

All doubles and men's singles games are played to 15 or 21 points, while women play to 11. Tie games may be *set* to an additional 2, 3 or 5 points, depending on the number of points in the game being played.

RACKET

STRINGS

T-PIECE

WT: 4-5 OZ.

FRAME/ HEAD

SHAFT

FERRULE

GRIP

HANDLE

CAP/BUTT END

COURT

SHORT SERVICE LINE

BACK BOUNDARY LINE/ SINGLES LONG SERVICE LINE

SIDE ALLEY (DOUBLES)

LEFT SERVICE COURT

BACK ALLEY/ DOUBLES SERVICE AREA

44'

2'6" WIDE

5'1" HIGH

POST

NET

17'

20'

DOUBLES LONG SERVICE LINE

CENTER LINE

RIGHT SERVICE COURT

SINGLES SIDE LINE

DOUBLES SIDE LINE

WT: 1/16 OZ.

RIBS

SKIRT 2-3/4"

WEIGHT

SHUTTLECOCK/ SHUTTLE/BIRD

BUTTON

1" DIA.

Baseball is played by two nine-man teams. The object of players on the batting team is to advance from home plate around the bases, in order, returning home. This is a *run*. The team scoring the most runs wins.

A game consists of nine innings. *Extra innings* are played to break a tie. Each team gets three outs in an inning. The team not at bat is on defense in the field. The visiting team bats first, at *the top* of each inning.

The pitcher throws to the batter. If the batter swings and misses, hits the pitch into foul territory or does not swing at a pitch in the strike zone, it is called a *strike*. Three strikes is an out. (Fouled third strikes are replayed). A batte

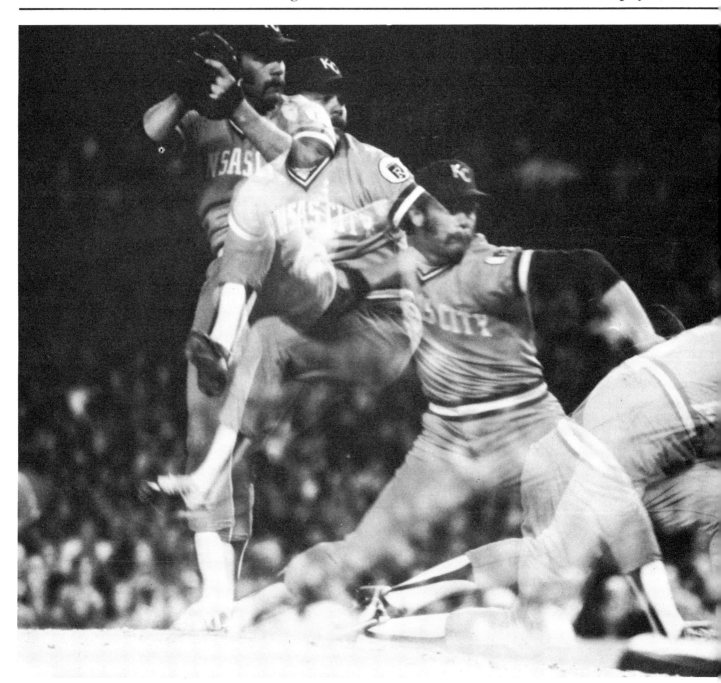

may also be put out by hitting a ball caught on the fly, or hitting the ball on the ground so that a fielder holding the ball touches first base before the batter steps on the base.

If the batter does not swing and the pitch is outside the strike zone, it is a ball. Four balls is a *walk*, *free pass* or *base on balls*, entitling the batter to go to first base, where he becomes a *runner*. A batted ball landing in fair territory so that the defense cannot put out the runner is a hit. If the batter reaches second on a hit it is a *double*, reaching third is a *triple*, circling the bases on one hit is a *home run*. Balls hit over the fence in fair territory on the fly are also home runs, entitling all runners on base to score.

PLAYER POSITIONS AND DIMENSIONS

BASEBALL SLANG

BASEBALL FIELD

Base runners are *safe* while touching a base and cannot be put out. Runners can be put out while off base if touched by a fielder holding the ball.

Runners may hold their base unless forced. *A force* occurs when all bases behind a runner are occupied and the runners on those bases are attempting to advance. (A runner on first is forced by the batter.) If a fielder holding the ball touches a base before a forced runner gets there, the runner is out.

A runner not forced can advance at his own risk on a batted ball. He may also *steal*, or run while the defense has the ball, advance on defensive misplays, or *errors*, on minor rules violations, or when forced by a walk.

LACES/BINDING
FINGERS
WELTING
WEBBING
THUMB
PALM
HEEL
POCKET
EYELETS
GLOVE MODEL

GLOVE/MITT

'MEAT'/SWEET SPOT
BAT
BARREL
LABEL/TRADEMARK
SIGNATURE/AUTOGRAPH
TAPE
42" (MAX.)
HANDLE
KNOB

STITCHES/LACES
COVER
9–9¼" CIR.
WT: 5–5¼ OZ.

BASEBALL/HORSEHIDE/'APPLE'

BATTING HELMET/HARD HAT
TEAM LOGO
UNDERSHIRT
PRE-GAME/BATTING PRACTICE JERSEY
BATTING GLOVE

SHELL
PADDING
CAGE
FACE MASK
THROAT PROTECTOR/'STEVIE'
UNIFORM SHIRT/BLOUSE
CHEST PROTECTOR

HIGH
17"
INSIDE
OUTSIDE
TRIM
PANTS
PIPING
INSIDE CORNER
MIDDLE
OUTSIDE CORNER
LOW

STRIKE ZONE

CATCHER'S MITT
STRAPS
WING
SHINGUARD
STIRRUP SOCK
SANITARY HOSE
CLEATS/SPIKES

CATCHER'S EQUIPMENT/ 'TOOLS OF IGNORANCE'

ANKLE EXTENSION

BATTING/HITTING/SWINGING

BATTING STANCE	BACKSWING AND STRIDE	SWING	CONTACT	FOLLOW-THROUGH

SCOREBOARD

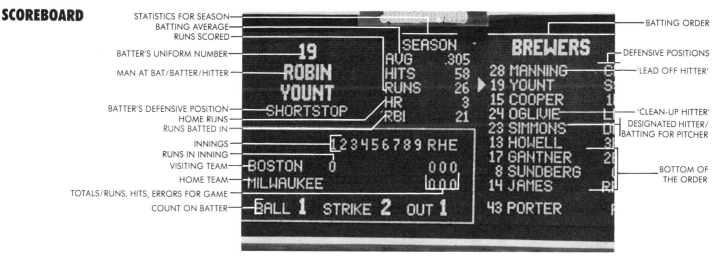

STATISTICS FOR SEASON
BATTING AVERAGE
RUNS SCORED
BATTER'S UNIFORM NUMBER
MAN AT BAT/BATTER/HITTER
BATTER'S DEFENSIVE POSITION
HOME RUNS
RUNS BATTED IN
INNINGS
RUNS IN INNING
VISITING TEAM
HOME TEAM
TOTALS/RUNS, HITS, ERRORS FOR GAME
COUNT ON BATTER

BATTING ORDER
DEFENSIVE POSITIONS
'LEAD OFF HITTER'
'CLEAN-UP HITTER'
DESIGNATED HITTER/
BATTING FOR PITCHER
BOTTOM OF
THE ORDER

19
ROBIN
YOUNT
SHORTSTOP

SEASON
AVG .305
HITS 58
RUNS 26
HR 3
RBI 21

BREWERS
28 MANNING
19 YOUNT
15 COOPER
24 OGLIVIE
23 SIMMONS
13 HOWELL
17 GANTNER
8 SUNDBERG
14 JAMES
43 PORTER

1 2 3 4 5 6 7 8 9 R H E
BOSTON   0   0 0 0
MILWAUKEE   0 0 0

BALL 1   STRIKE 2   OUT 1

Unlimited substituting is permitted, but replaced players cannot re-enter the game. Batters are often replaced by *pinch-hitters* and starting pitchers by *relief pitchers*.

Pitchers throw from a stretch, or set position with runners on base.

They use a variety of pitches and change speeds in an effort to prevent the batter from hitting.

There may be as few as one or as many as six umpires. The home plate umpire calls balls and strikes and runs the game. Base umpires

call safes and outs, fair and foul.

Some games for young players take place on down-sized fields. (Little League bases are 60′ apart). Some amateur and minor league games are shorter than nine innings.

FULL WIND-UP

| TAKE SIGNAL FROM CATCHER | PUMP | KICK/SWIVEL | STRIDE | RELEASE | FOLLOW-THROUGH |

STRETCH POSITION/SET POSITION

| TAKE SIGNAL FROM CATCHER | GRIP BALL | CHECK RUNNER | HOLD/SET | PUMP | KICK | RELEASE POINT | FOLLOW-THROUGH |
STRIDE

CURVE BALL

FORKBALL

KNUCKLEBALL

SLIDER

CHANGE UP/
CHANGE OF PACE

DROPPING
FASTBALL

RISING
FASTBALL

PITCHERS' GRIPS

UMPIRE'S SIGNALS

OUT/STRIKE

FOUL/TIME OUT

SAFE

SPECTATOR INTERFERENCE

FAIR BALL

FOUL TIP

MOVEMENT OF PITCHES

Ron Luciano

In this overhead view a rising ball gets larger, a sinking ball diminishes.

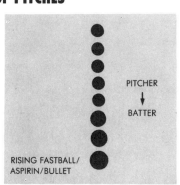

PITCHER → BATTER

RISING FASTBALL/ ASPIRIN/BULLET

PITCHER → BATTER

DROPPING FASTBALL

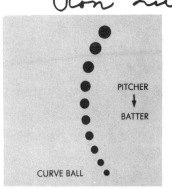

PITCHER → BATTER

CURVE BALL

PITCHER → BATTER

SCREWBALL

PITCHER → BATTER

SLIDER

PITCHER → BATTER

FORKBALL

PITCHER → BATTER

KNUCKLEBALL

BASKETBALL

Basketball is played indoors by two 5-player teams. Unlimited substitutions are permitted. American college and international games are played in two 20-minute halves. Professional games consist of four 12-minute quarters.

The object is to shoot an inflated rubber ball through the opponent's basket while preventing the other team from scoring at the opposite end. A *basket*, or *field goal*, scored from the floor is worth two points. In 'pro ball,' baskets made from

beyond the 3-point line are worth three points.

Free throws, or *foul shots*, are awarded by referees when a *foul*, usually illegal contact, is committed. The fouled player is given one or two uncontested throws from

COURT

'FLOOR'
BENCH
SCORER'S TABLE
SIDELINE
FOUL LINE/ FREE THROW LINE/ 'CHARITY' STRIPE
FREE-THROW CIRCLE
CENTER CIRCLE
BASKET
INTERNATIONAL FOUL LANE 19'
RESTRAINING CIRCLE
19'
FREE THROW LANE/KEY/ 3-SECOND LANE/'PAINT' 12' (COLLEGE) 16' (PRO)
LANE SPACE MARKS
50' (COLLEGE & PRO) 47¼' (INTERNATIONAL)
MIDCOURT LINE/ DIVISION LINE
BASE LINE/END LINE
3-POINT LINE
MIDCOURT/SUBSTITUTE BOX AREA
94' (COLLEGE & PRO) 85' (INTERNATIONAL)

JUMP SHOT

SHOT CLOCK/ 24-SECOND CLOCK
6'
BACKBOARD
GLASS
4'
RECTANGLE
BRACE MEMBER
18"
BASKET/ HOOP/ GOAL
15"-18"
SUPPORT UNIT
BASKETBALL
NET/CORDS
ATTACHMENT LOOPS
RIM/HOOP/RING/IRON
BACKPLATE
PLAYER'S SURNAME
GLENN 34
NUMBER
JERSEY
10'
COLUMN/ UPRIGHT/ STANCHION
SHORTS
PADDED BASE
SOCKS
SNEAKERS

DUNK/JAM/SLAM/STUFF

the foul line, worth one point if made.

The ball may be thrown, passed or dribbled. Players may take only one-and-a-half steps without dribbling, or bouncing the ball.

When a shot is missed, players vie for the ball as it bounds off the rim, or rebounds. The offensive team tries to slap it through the basket, a *tip in*, or regain control (*offensive rebound*) and maneuver for another shot. If the opposition gets the *defensive rebound*, it at-tempts to bring the ball upcourt to shoot at the other basket.

If a basket is scored, the defense inbounds from beneath its own basket. After a score or rebound, college and pro teams have 10 seconds to cross the midcourt line.

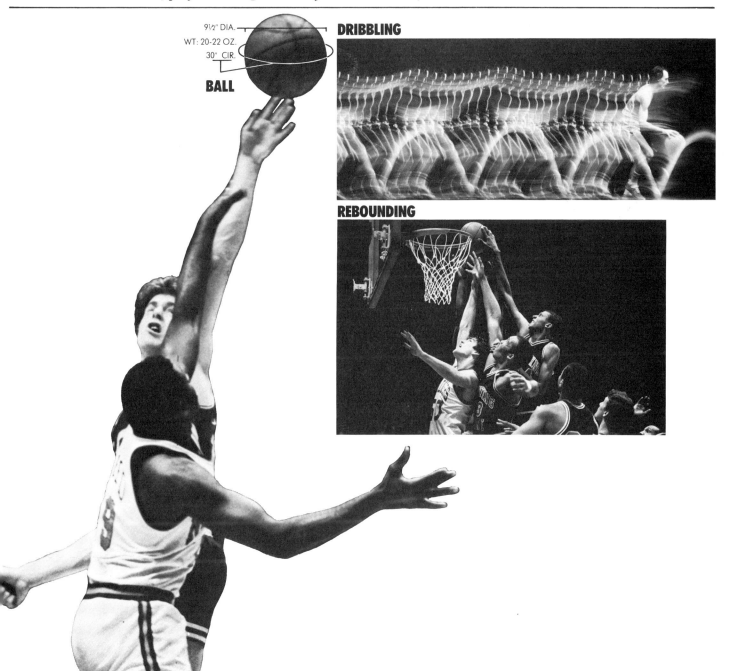

9½" DIA.
WT: 20-22 OZ.
30" CIR.

BALL

DRIBBLING

REBOUNDING

In pro basketball and some college leagues, a team has 24 seconds (30 in international play) from the time it gains possession to attempt a shot or it loses the ball.

Depending on the league, players may commit five or six *personal* *fouls*, for example, blocking, charging or pushing, before *fouling out*, before having to leave the game.

The basic shots are the dunk, in which a player leaps over the basket and slams the ball through it, the lay up, a shot bounced off the backboard from very close, the jump shot, attempted from long range, and the hook, in which a player pivots on one foot and hooks the ball over his head.

Two or three on-court *referees* or *umpires* officiate.

OFFICIALS' SIGNALS

NO BASKET/PLAY DOES NOT COUNT	3-PT. FIELD GOAL ATTEMPT	3-PT. ATTEMPT GOOD	PLAYER NUMBER COMMITTING FOUL	TIME OUT
OFFENSIVE FOUL/CHARGING	TRAVELING	HOLDING	ILLEGAL DRIBBLE/DOUBLE DRIBBLE	TECHNICAL FOUL
PUSHING	PERSONAL FOUL	BLOCKING	GOAL TENDING	HACKING/ ILLEGAL USE OF HANDS
DIRECTION OF PLAY	SCORE COUNTS & NUMBER OF FREE THROWS	OUT OF BOUNDS		

LAY UP

ZONE DEFENSES

Defensive players are responsible for protecting an area. The zone rotates as the ball is passed.

MAN-TO-MAN DEFENSES

Defensive players stay with their offensive counterpart wherever he or she goes.

John Wooden
JOHN WOODEN
FORMER HEAD COACH UCLA

1-2-2 ZONE

2-3 ZONE

Bobsledders race two-man or four-man *bobs*, or *sleds*, down a curving, narrow *chute* of solid ice through a minimum of 15 banked turns.

Events consist of four runs, or *heats*, over two or more days. The team with the lowest total time for all runs wins.

In both two-man '*boblets*' and four-man sleds, the crew's seats may be no more than 8″ off the ice.

Lead or iron *ballast* is often carried in sleds to bring them up to maximum weight.

Brakes are only used to stop at the completion of a run. Braking on the course results in automatic disqualification.

BOBRUN/COURSE

START

FINISH

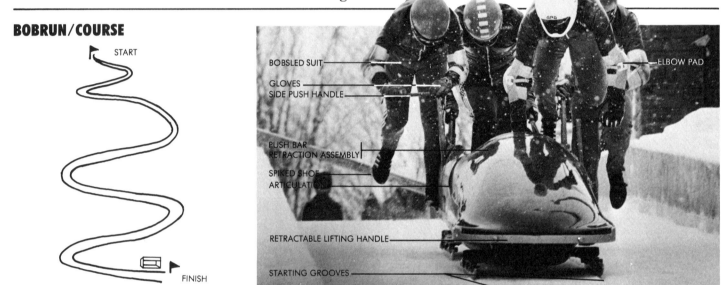

BOBSLED SUIT

GLOVES
SIDE PUSH HANDLE

PUSH BAR
RETRACTION ASSEMBLY

SPIKED SHOE
ARTICULATION

RETRACTABLE LIFTING HANDLE

STARTING GROOVES

ELBOW PAD

4-MAN BOBSLED

START

WALL

2'2¼" WIDE (MAX.)

ICE

DRIVER
NUMBER 2 MAN
NUMBER 3 MAN
BRAKEMAN

12'2' LONG (MAX.)

GOGGLES
HELMET

BRAKE HANDLE
CHASSIS
SIDE PUSH HANDLE
REINS/STEERING
CABLES
KINGPIN

PUSHER HANDLE
SHOCK ABSORBER
AIR SPRING

REAR BUMPER/
'BUNKS'
RUNNER SHOE
RUNNER TIP
BRAKEMAN'S SEAT
DRIVER'S SEAT BACK
DRIVER'S SEAT
STEERING RINGS
ARTICULATION JOINT
FRONT AND REAR
ARTICULATION MECHANISM
FRONT SHOCK ABSORBER
FRONT BUMPER SHOE
STEERING RATIO ADJUSTMENT
MAIN STEERING ARM/STEERING POST
BUMPER COWL

BOBSLED CUTAWAY

To start, the *pallino* is thrown by the team winning a coin toss.

A *frame* is completed when each player has rolled one ball, or *bocce*. A point is awarded at the end of the frame for each bocce nearer the pallino than an opponent's nearest ball.

Sixteen points wins team games, 11 individual games. A player may *spock*, or hit, an opponent's ball to score or decrease the opponent's total.

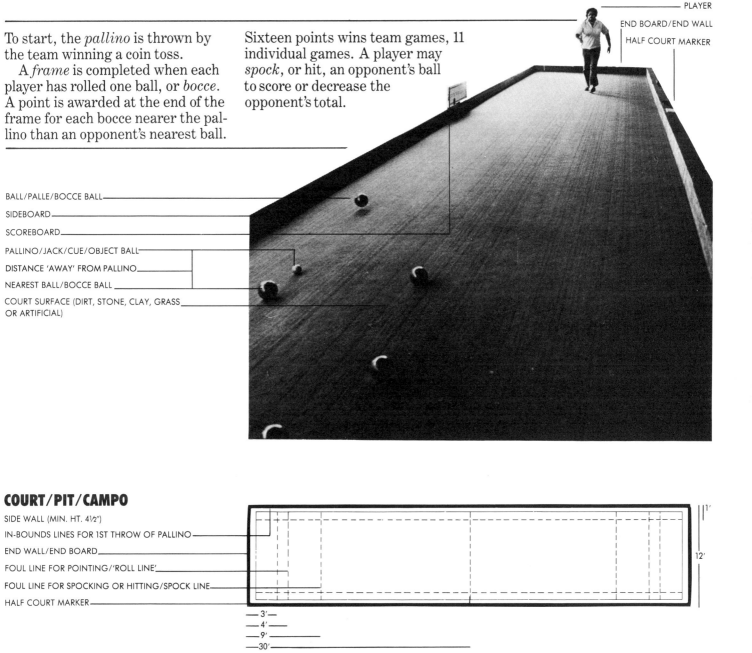

PLAYER
END BOARD/END WALL
HALF COURT MARKER

BALL/PALLE/BOCCE BALL
SIDEBOARD
SCOREBOARD
PALLINO/JACK/CUE/OBJECT BALL
DISTANCE 'AWAY' FROM PALLINO
NEAREST BALL/BOCCE BALL
COURT SURFACE (DIRT, STONE, CLAY, GRASS OR ARTIFICIAL)

COURT/PIT/CAMPO

SIDE WALL (MIN. HT. 4½")
IN-BOUNDS LINES FOR 1ST THROW OF PALLINO
END WALL/END BOARD
FOUL LINE FOR POINTING/'ROLL LINE'
FOUL LINE FOR SPOCKING OR HITTING/SPOCK LINE
HALF COURT MARKER

1'
12'

—3'—
—4'—
—9'—
—30'—

BALLS/EQUIPMENT

FULL TEAM'S BOCCE BALLS
DIA: 4⅜"-4½"

PALLINO/JACK/CUE/OBJECT BALL
DIA: 2⅛"-2½"

When judging a *physique contest*, the five to seven *judges* evaluate the *symmetry*, *muscularity* and *presentation* of the competitors.

Symmetry includes overall *balance* of body parts and muscle groups. Muscles must show rela-tively equal development and be in *harmony* with other body parts.

Muscularity includes *muscle size*, *development*, *definition* and *hardness*.

Presentation encompasses *grooming*, *posture*, *carriage*, *pro-jection* and *posing ability*.

In female contests, judges also score *choreography* and *grace*. Prior to appearing before judges on a *posing platform*, *'builders'* apply light oil to their bodies and work out to *'pump up'* their muscles in a

MANDATORY POSES JUDGING POINTS

BACK DOUBLE BICEPS POSE

ABDOMINALS POSE

SIDE TRICEPS POSE

SIDE-CHEST POSE

FREESTYLE ROUTINE/FREE POSING

varm-up room.

Competition begins with a *group facing* in which all entries in a class stand in a line and execute a series of *quarter-turns*. That is followed by *individual posing*, or *freestyle*, in which builders pose alone and perform a timed *full-posing routine*, including mandatory poses, to music. Last is *comparison posing*, in which all contestants are on stage and may be moved for easy comparison. The *meet winner* is chosen in a *posedown* of height or weight class winners.

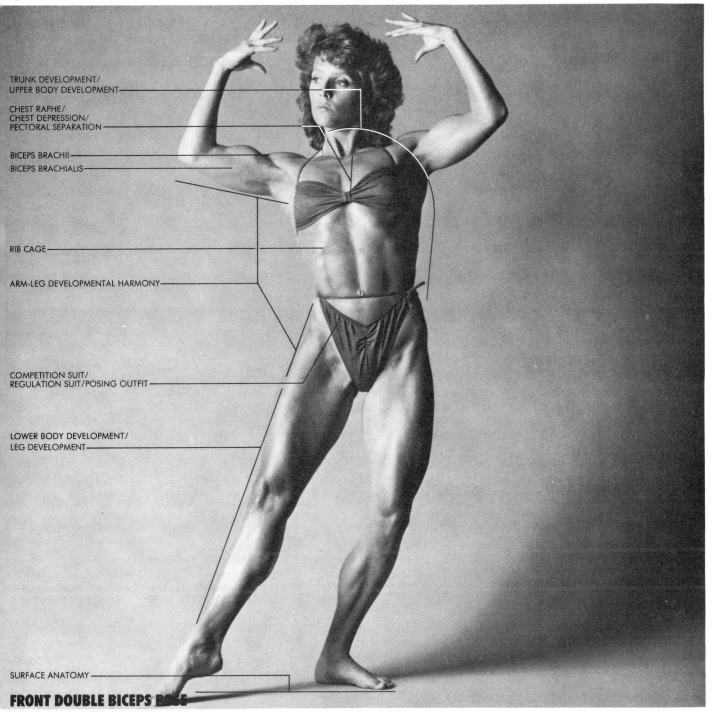

TRUNK DEVELOPMENT/
UPPER BODY DEVELOPMENT

CHEST RAPHE/
CHEST DEPRESSION/
PECTORAL SEPARATION

BICEPS BRACHII

BICEPS BRACHIALIS

RIB CAGE

ARM-LEG DEVELOPMENTAL HARMONY

COMPETITION SUIT/
REGULATION SUIT/POSING OUTFIT

LOWER BODY DEVELOPMENT/
LEG DEVELOPMENT

SURFACE ANATOMY

FRONT DOUBLE BICEPS POSE

A *game*, or *line*, consists of ten *frames*. A *bowler*, or *kegler*, gets two *rolls* in each frame. If all pins are knocked down on the first *shot* a *strike* (X), worth 10 plus the total pins knocked down on the next two balls, is scored. Knocking down all pins with two balls is a spare (/), worth 10 plus all pins knocked down on the next shot.

Candlepins and *duckpins* are forms of bowling with a lighter ball and smaller pins.

PIN-SETTER
BALL RETURN
PIN FINDER
RACK/SET-UP

LANES/ALLEYS

BALL RETURN CAPPING/'SUBWAY BALL RETURN'
SPOTS/TARGET ARROWS/MARKERS
BOARDS

GUIDES
CHANNEL/GUTTER

FOUL LINE
FOUL LIGHT/FOUL DETECTOR
APPROACH/RUNWAY

THUMB HOLE
SPAN
FINGER HOLE
BRIDGE
WEIGHT
WT: 10-16 LB.

BALL   **MOVEMENT OF BALL**

STRAIGHT BALL

CURVE BALL

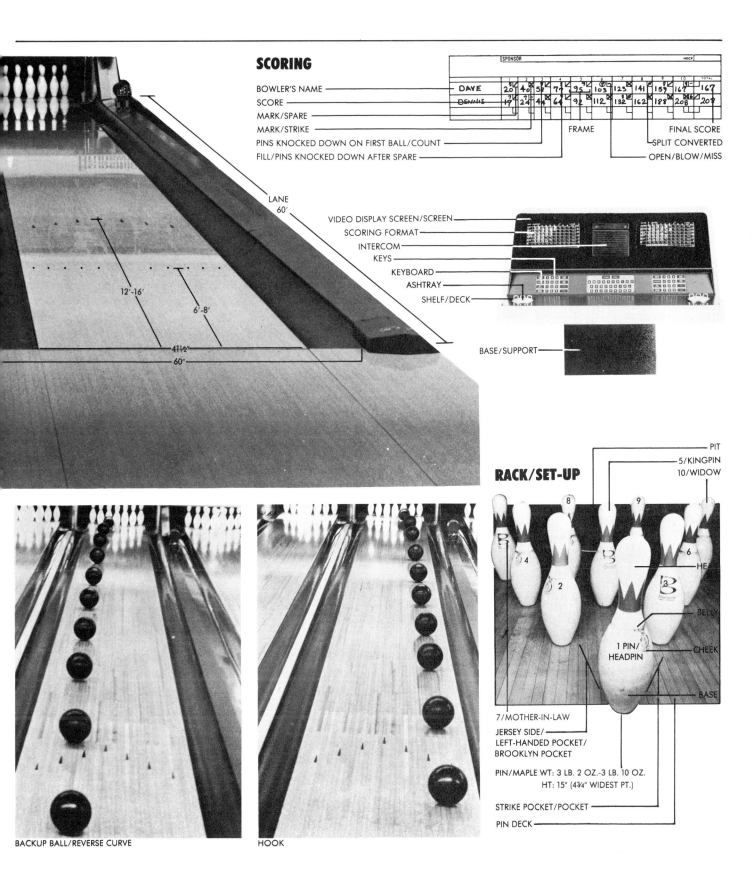

SCORING

BOWLER'S NAME
SCORE
MARK/SPARE
MARK/STRIKE
PINS KNOCKED DOWN ON FIRST BALL/COUNT
FILL/PINS KNOCKED DOWN AFTER SPARE

FRAME
FINAL SCORE
SPLIT CONVERTED
OPEN/BLOW/MISS

SPONSOR											HDCP	
	1	2	3	4	5	6	7	8	9	10		TOTAL
DAVE	20	40	59	77	95	103	125	141	159	167		167
DENNIS	17	24	44	64	92	112	132	162	188	208		208

LANE
60'

VIDEO DISPLAY SCREEN/SCREEN
SCORING FORMAT
INTERCOM
KEYS
KEYBOARD
ASHTRAY
SHELF/DECK

BASE/SUPPORT

12'-16'
6'-8'
41½"
60"

RACK/SET-UP

PIT
5/KINGPIN
10/WIDOW
8
9
4
5
6
2
HEEL
3
BELLY
1 PIN/
HEADPIN
CHEEK
BASE
7/MOTHER-IN-LAW
JERSEY SIDE/
LEFT-HANDED POCKET/
BROOKLYN POCKET

PIN/MAPLE WT: 3 LB. 2 OZ.-3 LB. 10 OZ.
HT: 15" (4¾" WIDEST PT.)

STRIKE POCKET/POCKET
PIN DECK

BACKUP BALL/REVERSE CURVE

HOOK

A boxing *match*, *bout* or *fight* is contested in three-minute *rounds*. The predetermined number of rounds, based on the level of competition, varies between three for amateur bouts and 15 for professional championships, or *title bouts*. A *timekeeper* sounds a *bell* to indicate the beginning and end of rounds. Between rounds boxers return to their corners for one-minute rests.

Boxers may only punch above the waistline and the front of the body.

Fights are decided by the judges' *decision*, by *retirement* (if a boxer concedes, or '*throws in the towel*'), by *disqualification* for fouling, by *knock out*, or by having the referee stop the fight, a *technical knock out*.

SCORECARD/CARD

BOXER/FIGHTER
COLOR OF TRUNKS
WINNER OF ROUND

Factors in Judging a Contest—
Ring Generalship
Effective Aggressiveness
Clean Hitting
Defense

Award Points on Following Observations:
1 Point —— Slightly Superior
2 Points —— Clearly Superior
3 Points —— Overwhelmingly Superior
4 Points —— Routed (One Sided)

ROUND JUDGED EVEN
NUMBER OF POINTS AWARDED
JUDGE'S SIGNATURE

BOXING RING/PRIZE RING

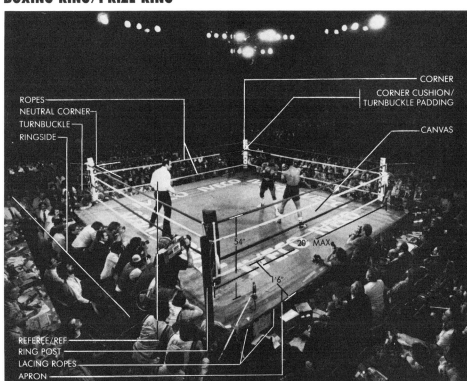

ROPES
NEUTRAL CORNER
TURNBUCKLE
RINGSIDE

CORNER
CORNER CUSHION/
TURNBUCKLE PADDING

CANVAS

54"
20" MAX
6"

REFEREE/REF
RING POST
LACING ROPES
APRON

AMATEUR BOXERS

HEADGEAR/HEADGUARD

TANK TOP/T-SHIRT
BOXING GLOVE
GLOVE HITTING SURFACE
TRUNKS

BOXING SHOE/BOOT

SWEAT SOCK

In pro boxing the judges' decision may be based on the number of rounds awarded to a fighter or the total number of points the fighter has won in a bout. When all judges vote for the same boxer it is called a *unanimous decision*. A fighter winning by majority vote wins a *split decision*.

A knockout, or *KO*, occurs when a fighter is beaten to the canvas and cannot rise before the referee counts to 10. A technical knockout, or *TKO*, occurs when the ref stops the fight.

Most amateur fights are judged on a *20-point must system*. The winner of a round is given 20 points, the loser receives fewer, depending on performance. The fighter with the most points wins.

BOXING SLANG

THE ATTIC/UPSTAIRS/BELFRY
COBWEBS
GLASS JAW/
CHINA CHIN/
CEMENT CHIN
MOUSE/SHINER
PUG NOSE
CAULIFLOWER
 EAR
BUTTON

PUG/
PUGILIST/
PALOOKA/
GLADIATOR

BANDAGES/WRAPPER
DUKE/KNUCKLE SANDWICH
BREADBASKET/LABONZA/
 LUNCH BOX
BELT
SOUTH OF THE BORDER/
 DOWNSTAIRS
GROIN

FIGHTER'S CORNER

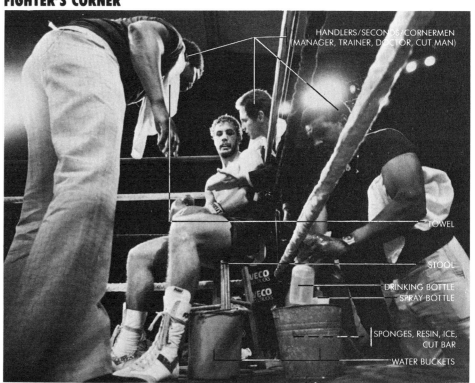

HANDLERS/SECONDS/CORNERMEN
(MANAGER, TRAINER, DOCTOR, CUT MAN)

TOWEL
STOOL
DRINKING BOTTLE
SPRAY BOTTLE
SPONGES, RESIN, ICE,
 CUT BAR
WATER BUCKETS

SPARRING EQUIPMENT

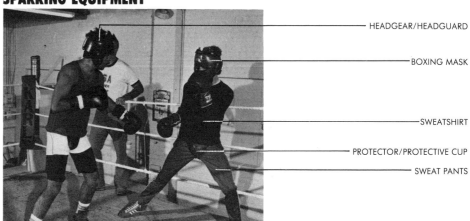

HEADGEAR/HEADGUARD
BOXING MASK
SWEATSHIRT
PROTECTOR/PROTECTIVE CUP
SWEAT PANTS

Amateur boxing places greater emphasis on boxing skills than does pro fighting. The hitting surface of the glove is painted to help judges determine how many *scoring blows* are landed. A *knockdown* is credited as an effective blow, only worth a certain number of points.

Fouls in pro and amateur bouts result in points being deducted, as well as disqualification.

There are between two and five voting judges.

Fighters compete in one of 14 *weight divisions* or *classes*. Among them are *flyweights* (below 112 lb.), *bantamweights* (112-118), *lightweights* (126-135), *welterweights* (135-147), *middleweights* (147-160), *light-heavyweights* (160-175) and *heavyweights* (unlimited).

PUNCHES & STRATEGIES

STRAIGHT LEFT

ROUNDHOUSE/ OVERHAND RIGHT

LEFT JAB/DEFENSE 'SLIPS' THE PUNCH

LEFT HOOK

UPPERCUT

RIGHT CROSS

CLINCH/TIE UP

FOULS

HITTING ON BACK OF NECK/RABBIT PUNCH

HITTING BELOW THE BELT

HITTING ON THE BACK/KIDNEY PUNCH

HITTING WITH OPEN GLOVE

HITTING A MAN WHO IS DOWN

BUTTING

HITTING ON BACK OF HEAD OR SHOULDER, OR WRESTLING

International competition is conducted in one-man, two-man and seven-man Canadian canoes, and in one-man, two-man and four-man kayaks. *Canoeists* and *kayakers*, also known as *kayakists*, compete on *flat water courses* in *sprint races* (500 and 1,000 meters) and *distance races* (5,000 and 10,000 meters).

In championship starts, officials hold the boats so that their sterns are touching the starting pontoons. An *aligner* raises a white flag when all boats are level and stationary. A start then takes place.

In sprints, boats race straight and must remain in their lanes from start to finish. In distance races, boats may leave their lanes but must return to them for the last 1,000 meters. During distance

CANOE/
CANADIAN CANOE/
ALASKAN CANOE

STERN THWART
STERN

GRIP
SHAFT
THROAT — PADDLE
BLADE

FRONT THWART

DELTA-FORM HULL

BOW COAMING

DECK

BOW

FOOT BRACE   GUNWALE   KNEE PAD

races, one canoe may position itself so that it rides on an opponent's bow wave, a maneuver called *wash hanging*.

In Canadian canoes *paddlers* kneel in the open boats and *J stroke* with a single-bladed paddle. The twisting stroke maneuvers the boat in a straight line. Kayakers propel their craft with a *double-bladed paddle* and guide them with a *foot-controlled rudder*.

All boats must meet maximum and minimum requirements. The one-man canoe, for example, may be no longer than 17'7" and weigh no more than 35 pounds.

Competitors may be disqualified for a variety of infractions, but a capsize always results in elimination.

KAYAK

STERN · AFT DECK · SHAFT · BLADES · PADDLE · FOREDECK · BOW

COCKPIT · ADJUSTABLE SEAT · COAMING/COCKPIT RIM/ SPLASH GUARD · ADJUSTABLE BOLT

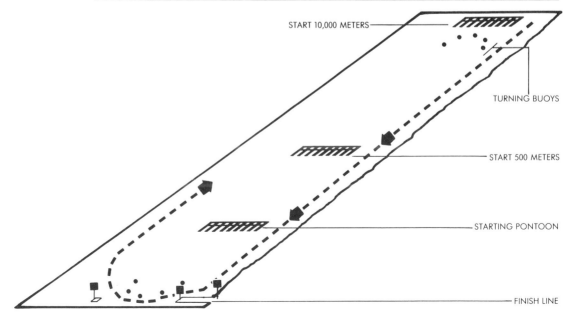

OLYMPIC RACE COURSE

START 10,000 METERS · TURNING BUOYS · START 500 METERS · STARTING PONTOON · FINISH LINE

In *whitewater canoe races*, one- and two-man kayaks, two-man canoes (decked over with individual *cockpits*) and open canoes, paddled solo or by two-man teams, compete on rapid river courses.

Contestants must navigate 25 to 30 *control gates*, pairs of poles suspended just above the water, in the correct order and direction, sometimes by reversing, paddling back through an *eddy*, or driving through a series of large standing waves, called *haystacks*.

Penalty points, in the form of seconds subtracted from elapsed time, are imposed for touching gates, failure to negotiate them in the proper direction, or for missing them entirely.

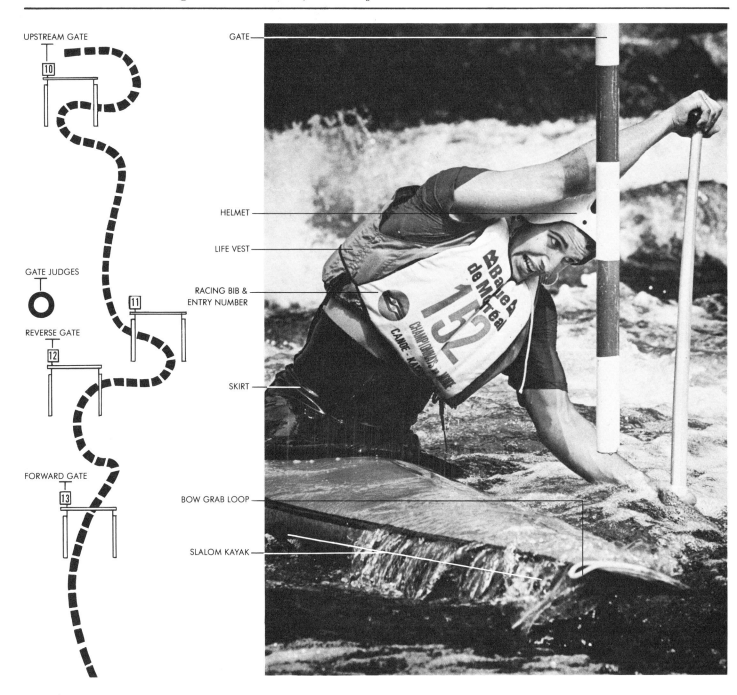

UPSTREAM GATE

10

GATE JUDGES

REVERSE GATE

12

11

FORWARD GATE

13

GATE

HELMET

LIFE VEST

RACING BIB & ENTRY NUMBER

SKIRT

BOW GRAB LOOP

SLALOM KAYAK

Cricket is played by two teams of 11 *cricketers* each, with one team in the field, the other at bat. The bowler, at one wicket, throws, or *bowls*, to the batsman at the other in such a way that the ball bounces in front of the wicket. If the ball knocks the bails off the wicket, or if it hits the batsman standing directly in front of the wicket, the batsman is out. The batsman, or *striker*, tries to hit the ball away from *fieldsmen* so that he and a batsman stationed at the other wicket, the *non-striker*, may exchange places. Each exchange is one *run*. Once a bowler has bowled six balls at one wicket, called an *over*, a teammate bowls to the batsman at the opposite wicket.

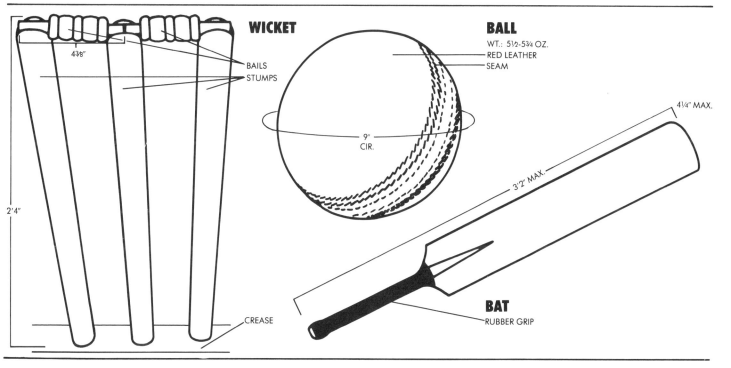

WICKET

4⅜"

BAILS
STUMPS

2'4"

CREASE

BALL

WT.: 5½-5¾ OZ.
RED LEATHER
SEAM

9"
CIR.

4¼" MAX.

3'2" MAX.

BAT
RUBBER GRIP

BOWLER

BATSMAN

WICKETKEEPER

SWEATER

BATSMAN'S GLOVES
THIGH PROTECTOR
WHITE FLANNELS

BAT

LEG GUARDS

WICKETKEEPER'S GLOVES

WICKET

LEG GUARD

BOOT
BALL

CREASE 4' WIDE

BOWLING CREASE

A batsman may be put out by having a hit ball caught in the air, by allowing a bowled ball to knock the bails off the wicket behind him, or having a fieldsman similarly 'break' the wicket behind him with the ball while he is running between wickets. Batsmen do not have to run on hit balls.

As each batsman is put out a new man takes his place until 10 of a team's players have been put out. That ends a team's *inning*. Major matches usually consist of two innings, played over two or three days, with breaks for lunch and tea.

The captain of the fielding team, and the bowler, decide in which, of many field positions, to place the fieldsmen.

CRICKET GROUND & FIELDING POSITIONS

UMPIRE SIGNALS

OUT   NO BALL   ONE SHORT   LEG BYE   SIX RUNS   FOUR RUNS

CROQUET

A toss determines the allocation of the four colors. These colors are painted on the stake, or peg, and control the order of play. Players use balls of the color allocated to them. The first *striker* hits the ball with his mallet at the balkline. Sub-sequent strikers do likewise. The course leads through the wickets, or hoops, toward the stake, with strikers alternating turns. A striker makes a *roquet* by knocking his ball into an opponent's. A ball through the proper wicket in the proper direction scores a point. Winners are decided by total points or by order of course completion. There are two courses: nine wickets and two stakes, or six wickets and one stake.

COURT

NORTH BALKLINE

105 FT.

SOUTH BALKLINE

84 FT.

BALL

EXTENSION/SPIRE

PEG/STAKE

COLORS/ORDER OF PLAY

MALLET

HANDLE/GRIP

SHAFT

HEAD

FACE

CROWN

CLIP/MARKER

UPRIGHT

JAWS

WICKET/HOOP

A curling team, or *rink*, consists of four players, led by a captain, or *skip*. The game is played on a lane of ice called a rink, or *sheet*. A player slides his stone, or rock, toward a *tee* at the center of the house, also called a *head* or *goal*.

Sweepers use brooms to alter the speed, or *weight*, of the stone and its direction, *curl* or *bend*.

Teams alternate, with each player *delivering* two stones. The 16 deliveries make up one *end*, or *inning*. A point is awarded for each of a team's stones that is closer to the tee than the opponents' nearest stone. A game consists of any prearranged number of ends, usually 10 or 12. The team with the most points wins.

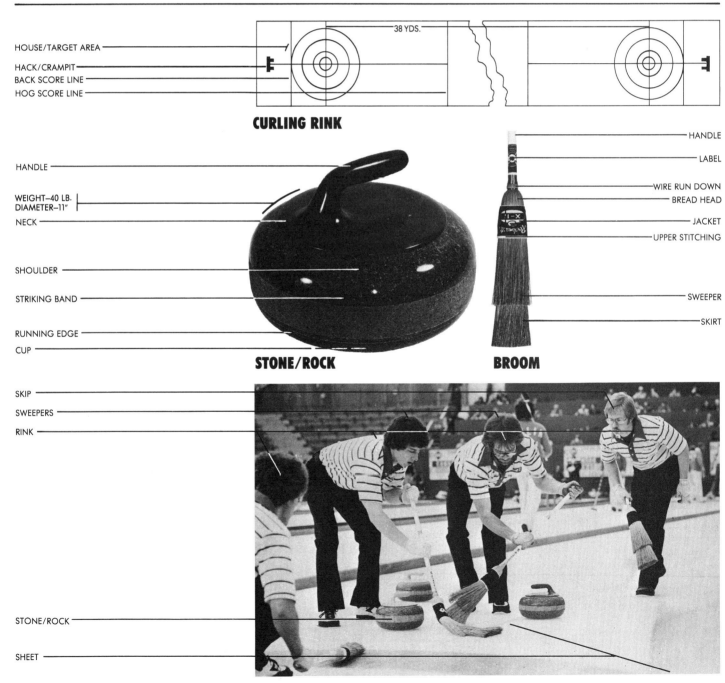

HOUSE/TARGET AREA

HACK/CRAMPIT
BACK SCORE LINE
HOG SCORE LINE

38 YDS.

CURLING RINK

HANDLE

WEIGHT—40 LB.
DIAMETER—11"

NECK

SHOULDER

STRIKING BAND

RUNNING EDGE

CUP

STONE/ROCK

HANDLE

LABEL

WIRE RUN DOWN
BREAD HEAD

JACKET
UPPER STITCHING

SWEEPER

SKIRT

BROOM

SKIP

SWEEPERS

RINK

STONE/ROCK

SHEET

Cycle racing is divided into track and road events. Track racers compete at various distances in *pursuits*, in which racers start at opposite sides of the track and try to overtake each other (if racers are not caught, the *rider* covering a specified distance first wins), *time trials*, one rider against the clock, and *sprints*, in which two or three cyclists race over one or more laps. Timing is over the last 200 meters, so earlier laps are used to gain the inside position.

Track bikes have lightweight *frames*, one gear and no brakes.

Road races may take place over hundreds of miles and many days. They are often raced in *stages*, in which competitors cover a specified number of miles per day.

ROAD RACING BIKE

PADDED HELMET
CHIN STRAP
SLEEVED JERSEY
DARK-COLORED RACING SHORTS
STEM
BRAKE LEVER
DROPPED HANDLEBAR
FRONT BRAKE CABLE
REAR BRAKE CABLE
SHIFTERS
REAR BRAKE
FRONT BRAKE
FORK/FORK BLADE
WATER BOTTLE HOLDER
CHAIN RING
FRONT HUB
FRONT WHEEL QUICK RELEASE
CHAIN STAY
TOE CLIP
TOE STRAP
PEDAL
DRIVE CHAIN
REAR DERAILLEUR

RACING SHOE

EYELET FACING
MESH TOP
SOLE
CLEAT
VENTILATION HOLES

VELODROME/RACING TRACK

567'

294'

23'

START/FINISH LINE
TUNNEL ENTRANCE
33° BANKED TURNS

JUDGES' TOWER
GRANDSTANDS

LIGHTS
CONCRETE TRACK

INFIELD/WARM UP AREA
SAFETY LINE
BALUSTRADE/FENCE

INDIVIDUAL PURSUIT & TIME TRIAL FLAT

TRACK BIKE

TIRE
RIM
SPOKES
UPRIGHT HANDLEBARS
FORK
HEAD TUBE

BOLT-ON PEDAL
DOWNTUBE
CROSS BAR/TOP TUBE
SEAT TUBE
SEAT
SEAT STAY
HELMET/SHELL

Darts, or *darting*, is played by individuals, pairs or teams of any number. In *tournament darts*, the most universally played game, individuals start with 301 points. In team play, the *opening score* may be increased to 501 or 1,001. Sides take turns throwing three darts. The score from each *throw* is subtracted from the remaining total. The first side to reduce its score to exactly zero wins. Each game is called a *leg*. Three legs win a match.

Other *clockface games* include *round-the-clock, all fives, scrubbers* (also called *cricket), baseball, high score, killer, Mulligan, sudden death,* and *Shanghai.*

DART

FLIGHT

SHAFT

BARREL

POINT

DART BOARD/ENGLISH CLOCK

1'6"

TRIPLE RING/
TRIPLE-SCORE RING

DOUBLE BULL'S EYE/
50-POINT RING

DOUBLE RING/
DOUBLE-SCORE RING

BULL'S EYE/25-POINT RING

SECTORS/
SINGLE-SCORE RINGS

NO SCORING RING

SCOREBOARD

SCOREKEEPER

5'8"

8'

THROWING LINE/
HOCKEY LINE/
TOE LINE

Fancy diving, the formal name for the sport of diving, consists of intricate in-air maneuvers culminating with a graceful entry into the water. There are four events: platform and springboard competitions for men and women.

Men are judged on 11 dives, women on 10. *Preliminary contests* are held when there are more than 16 divers. The eight divers with the most points advance to the final round where they perform the same dives they executed in the

preliminary.

Each dive has a preassigned *degree of difficulty* coefficient, or *DD*. Thus, dives range in numerical value from 1.2, for a simple forward dive, to 3.5 for a highly difficult *forward 4 1/2 somersault.*

DIVING POOL/TANK

10-METER PLATFORM/ HIGHBOARD (33')

DIVERS' ELEVATOR

7.5-METER PLATFORM (24'5")

5-METER PLATFORM (16'3")

3-METER PLATFORM (9'9")

THE TOWER

3-METER SPRINGBOARD (9'9")

1-METER SPRINGBOARD (3'3")

MECHANICAL SURFACE AGITATION

JUDGES

DIVING TANK (17' DEEP)

PRACTICE BOARDS/WARM-UP BOARDS

A panel of seven judges awards points for each dive, as follows: failed dive—0; unsatisfactory—½-2; deficient—2½-4½; satisfactory—5-6; good—6½-8; very good—8½-10. The highest and lowest scores are discarded and the remaining five are multiplied first by ⅗, then by the dive's degree of difficulty to determine the final score for the dive. The winner of each event is the diver with the greatest number of points.

Divers lose points for restarting a running dive, touching the end of the board, diving to the side of the direct line of flight, or entering the water 'short' or 'over' (less than or beyond the 90-degree entry angle).

COMPONENTS OF A DIVE & JUDGING POINTS

EXECUTION
COMPONENTS OF VARIOUS POSITIONS PERFORMED CRISPLY, WITH FLAIR & CONTROL, LEGS TOGETHER, FINGERS & TOES POINTED, POSITIONS HELD LONG ENOUGH TO BE CLEARLY IDENTIFIED

HURDLE

TAKE OFF
BOLD, REASONABLY HIGH AND CONFIDENT, LEAVING FROM BOTH FEET SIMULTANEOUSLY

STARTING POSITION
BODY STRAIGHT, HEAD ERECT, ARMS TO THE SIDES

RUN
STRAIGHT, TAKEN WITHOUT HESITATION, LEADING SMOOTHLY INTO THE HURDLE

ENTRY
VERTICAL, BODY STRAIGHT, FEET TOGETHER, TOES POINTED, ARMS STRETCHED BEYOND THE HEAD, HANDS CLOSE TOGETHER

Dives are divided into the six *groups* illustrated below. The first five dive groups are practiced on the springboard. All six are contested in platform diving. A twist dive is a forward, backward, reverse or inward dive, combined with a twist.

Dives in each group may be performed in one of many *positions*—straight, with no bends at waist, hips or knees; pike, bent at the waist only; tuck, with body bent at the knees, hips and waist; free, a combination of straight, pike or

tuck, also used in certain twisting dives.

Running dives begin when the diver takes the first step of his *run*. *Standing dives* begin at the front end of the platform.

A forward dive in the pike posi-

FORWARD DIVE

STRAIGHT POSITION

INWARD DIVE
(INWARD 1½ SOMERSAULT)

TUCK POSITION

BACKWARD DIVE
(FLYING BACK SOMERSAULT)

STRAIGHT POSITION

FREE POSITION

TUCK POSITION

tion is also called a *jackknife*, just as a forward dive in a straight, or *layout*, position is often referred to as a *swan dive*. A somersault is a *flip*, a reverse dive is a *gainer*, or *Mohlberg*, and an improper form of landing is a *bellyflop*.

Entering the water with virtually no splash is a *rip entry*, accomplished by landing on the palms of the hands and opening the water with them. In addition, the diver may perform a breaststroke motion with his arms underwater, thereby creating pockets of air on either side and vanishing through the vacuum between them, leaving only puddles of foam on the surface.

REVERSE DIVE

PIKE POSITION

TWIST DIVE

HALF TWIST

ARMSTAND DIVE

CUT THROUGH

Although much recreational diving is done with *scuba*, an acronym for *self-contained underwater breathing apparatus*, competitive events usually involve *breathhold diving*, or *free diving*, without equipment.

In spearfishing tournaments, contested by men and women, pairs, mixed pairs and juniors, points are accrued by *spearfishermen*, or *spearfishers*, for the number of fish species taken and their size. In *underwater*

hockey, breathhold divers compete with sticks and balls, in much the same way as field hockey players.

Navigation contests, in which individual skills are tested underwater, are conducted with scuba equipment.

SCUBA DIVER

- SNORKEL
- MASK/ FACE MASK
- LENS
- SKIRT
- STRAP
- AIR HOSE/ REGULATOR HOSE
- REGULATOR MOUTHPIECE
- INFLATION HOSE
- BC INFLATOR MOUTHPIECE
- BUOYANCY COMPENSATOR/ FLOTATION DEVICE
- AUTO INFLATION HOSE
- WET SUIT JACKET
- PRESSURE GAUGE HOSE
- LEAD WEIGHT
- COMPASS
- GLOVE
- POCKET
- WEIGHT BELT
- DIVER'S WATCH/ SUBMERSIBLE WATCH/ DIVE TIMER
- KNIFE
- PRESSURE GAUGE
- DEPTH GAUGE
- SHEATH
- WET SUIT PANTS
- BOOT/BOOTIE
- HEEL STRAP
- SIDE RAIL
- FOOT POCKET
- VENT
- RIB
- BLADE
- FIN/ SWIM FIN/ FLIPPER

SPEAR GUN

- SAFETY
- RUBBER BANDS
- TRIGGER MECHANISM
- HANDLE
- SLIDE SPRING
- WISHBONE
- NOTCHES
- BUTT
- DOUBLE BARB TIP
- TIP GUARD
- SHAFT
- SIGHT
- MUSSLE
- SHOCK CORD
- BARREL STOCK
- SHOCK CORD RELEASE FINGER
- GRIP
- BUTT STOCK

A greyhound race begins when an *electrically operated lure* passes *starting boxes* holding seven to nine greyhounds. The male *dogs* and female *bitches* are released to chase the *'rabbit'* around an oval course.

Coursing greyhounds are regis-tered in a *stud book* and identified on a *bertillion card*, which is used by *Paddock Judges* to prevent ille-gal substitution. Greyhounds are rated by performance on the track into six categories, *A,B,C,D,E*, and *M* (Maiden.) A *Maiden* is a grey-hound who has never won a race. Greyhounds race in category and are raised or lowered depending on finish over a few consecutive races.

3/8 MILE COURSE START

7/16 MILE COURSE START

BACKSTRETCH

INFIELD

FINISH LINE

5/16 MILE COURSE START

RACETRACK

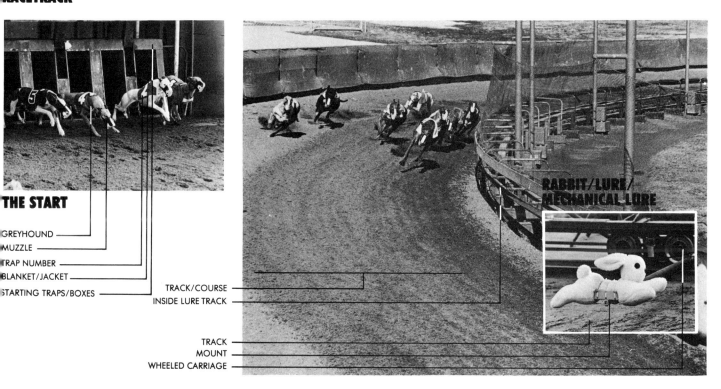

THE START

GREYHOUND

MUZZLE

TRAP NUMBER

BLANKET/JACKET

STARTING TRAPS/BOXES

TRACK/COURSE

INSIDE LURE TRACK

TRACK

MOUNT

WHEELED CARRIAGE

RABBIT/LURE/ MECHANICAL LURE

BERTILLION CARD/IDENTITY CARD

STORMY RANCHER — Wt+Bl Bd D

Name	Wt.	Color	Sex	Whelping Date		Sire	Dam

COLORATION AND MARKINGS

SEX ('D' DENOTES DOG)

52A   2642Q   Smkair

TATTOO NUMBERS

RIGHT HIND FOOT   LEFT HIND FOOT   NAILS   TOES

WHELPING DATE

FATHER

MOTHER

RIGHT SIDE   LEFT SIDE

TOES   NAILS

RIGHT FRONT FOOT   LEFT FRONT FOOT

TOENAIL COLOR

FRANK
Recorded Owner   Date   Vol.   Number

This Bertillion is the property of
MILE HIGH KENNEL CLUB
DENVER, COLO.

FORM NO. 1

Greyhounds look pretty much alike to most people, but each animal has distinguishing markings. Every hound on a racing list, then, has its own bertillion card. This identity card includes the greyhound's name, coloration and markings, sex ('Dog' denotes a male), owner, and tattoo numbers. Coloration and all markings are drawn in detail, even to include the color of the toenails.

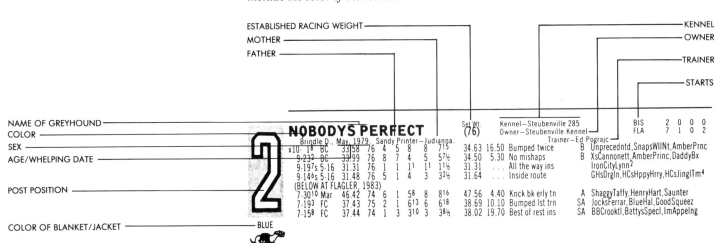

ESTABLISHED RACING WEIGHT ——————————— KENNEL

MOTHER ——————————— OWNER

FATHER ——————————— TRAINER

——————————— STARTS

NAME OF GREYHOUND

COLOR

SEX

AGE/WHELPING DATE

POST POSITION

COLOR OF BLANKET/JACKET

NOBODYS PERFECT   Set Wt.   Kennel—Steubenville 285   BIS   2 0 0 0
Brindle D., May, 1979, Sandy Printer—Judianna.   (76)   Owner—Steubenville Kennel   FLA   7 1 0 2
                                        Trainer—Ed Pograjc

x10- 1⁸	BC	33⅝58	76	4	5	8	8	7¹⁵	34.63	16.50	Bumped twice	B	Unprecednt, SnapsWllNt, AmberPrnc
9-23³	BC	33⅝99	76	8	7	4	5	57½	34.50	5.30	No mishaps	B	XsCannonett, AmberPrinc, DaddyBx
9-19⁷s	5-16	31.31	76	1	1	1¹	1¹	1¹½	31.31	. . .	All the way ins		IronCityLynn²
9-14⁶s	5-16	31.48	76	1	4	3	3	32½	31.64	. . .	Inside route		GHsDrgln, HCsHppyHrry, HCsJinglTm⁴
(BELOW AT FLAGLER, 1983)
7-30¹⁰	Mar	46.42	74	6	1	5⁸	8	8¹⁶	47.56	4.40	Knck bk erly tn	A	ShaggyTaffy, HenryHart, Saunter
7-19³	FC	37.43	75	2	1	6¹³	6	6¹⁸	38.69	10.10	Bumped 1st trn	SA	JocksFerrar, BlueHal, GoodSqueez
7-15⁸	FC	37.44	74	1	3	3¹⁰	3	3⁸½	38.02	19.70	Best of rest ins	SA	BBCrooktl, BettysSpecl, ImAppelng

BLUE

RACING PROGRAM

RACING FORM

Howard Haley's Light Brindle D.
January 19, 1981. Detroit City*—Daddy's Date.

Little Howard	12.00	4.20	4.20	Trif. 1-4-7—$287.60
Neka Jones		3.00	2.60	Quin. 1-4—$20.40
IV's Captain			3.80	

2nd RACE—5-16 MILE   GRADE BB   TIME: 31.48

2-1¹¹	Unwindable	67	6	6	4	2	1¹½	31.48	5.50
1-31¹¹	Four Stroke	69	3	3	1³	1¹	2¹½	31.57	2.50
2-1⁴	River Moss	68	2	7	6	4	3¹½	31.64	11.70
1-31⁴	Pat C Streaker	66	8	1	2	3	4²½	31.60	2.50
1-31¹⁰	Fire In The Hole	70	1	4	5	5	5⁵½	31.87	16.80
2-1⁴	Dutch D West	66	4	8	7	7	6⁸½	32.06	14.20
2-1⁴	Another Dollar	59	5	5	8	8	7¹⁰	32.18	3.10
1-31¹⁰	Dane Hunter	73	7	2	3	6	8¹²	32.34	15.60

PAST PERFORMANCE CHART

Date and Race Previous Event	Distance	Track Condition	Time of Winner	Weight at Post Time	Post Position	Start	One-Eighth Lengths Back	Stretch Call	Finish—Lengths From Winner	Actual Running Time	Odds	Comment	Grade	Order of Finish	
4-21¹¹	5/16m	F	30⁸⁴	71	6	8	5	4	4⁸	31⁵³	4.50	Blkd 1st, closed	[A]	ProudBeauty ChfDan George DQ'sTurry	8
4-16⁸	5/16m	F	31³⁷	71½	8	5	5	3⁸	3⁸	31⁸⁸	10.40	Blkd early, rcvrd	[A]	JR'sMelissa PrideEckert DaleMRector	8
x4-13⁸	5/16m	F	31⁸³	71	8	1⁸	1⁴	1¹⁸	31¹²	1.50*	In full command	[B]	WorldFree RenoGMC LadyJontue	8
4- 8¹²	5/16m	F	32⁸²	71	4	7	5	3¹²	32²³	1.60*	Much trble, rcvrd	[B]	KASlumber ElectronicPwr BogusCash	8
4- 3⁶	5/16m	F	31¹⁸	70	1	4	1	1²	1⁴²	31¹⁰	7.40	Backstretch drive	[C]	JR'sWineta LC'sLadyAnn SlickJocker	8
x3-30¹	5/16m	F	30⁸³	71	7	6	1³	1	1²²	30⁸³	6.00	Cleared, 1st turn	[D]	SpotOfMusic ColorSargeant PowerTrip	8

Equestrianism, the training of horses for specific tasks, is contested in show jumping, dressage, and eventing, also called *horse trials* of the *three-day event*.

Show jumping takes place in an arena. *Riders* direct their *mounts* over 12-15 *obstacles* which range in height from 2'6" to 7'2" and are placed on a course 763 to 981 yards long.

Hunter class horses are judged primarily on style, grace and the compatibility of horse and rider.

Open Jumpers are judged solely on their ability to clear fences. The horse with the fewest *faults* over a prescribed number of runs wins.

Faults include refusing to jump, knocking down a rail and exceeding the time limit for a run.

COURSE

HARD HAT/
HUNT CAP
RIDING SHIRT/
RAT CATCHER'
BRIDLE

COAT
BREECHES
BOOTS
SPURS

ENGLISH SADDLE
SADDLE PAD

SHOW JUMPING

SHOW JUMPING FENCES

UPRIGHT/GATE

UPRIGHT/STONE WALL

COMBINATION JUMP/IN AND OUT

WATER JUMP

WATER JUMP

SPREAD/CROSS BARS

SPREAD/OXER

SPREAD/PARALLEL POLES

SPREAD/PARALLEL POLES

TRIPLE BARS/STAIRCASE

Dressage, or *schooling*, tests the ability of the horse and rider to perform a variety of specific movements which demonstrate control, *pace, seat* (rider's posture), fluidity and ease of movement.

Five judges around the arena score each movement from zero to 10.

Competitors have 10-12 minutes to complete a 30-movement *test*. These include command of the *natural gaits* (walk, trot, canter) and numerous variations (including the *piaffe*, an elegant trot in place, and *passage*, the same trot but with forward movement), *transitions* between paces, *halts* and *pirouettes* (turns done with the horse's hind legs remaining in place.)

There is both individual and team competition.

TURNOUT FOR HORSE AND RIDER

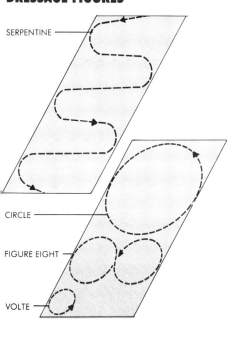

TOP HAT
ASCOT
BRAIDED MANE
RIDING GLOVES
REINS

FORMAL JACKET/
SWALLOWTAIL JACKET
BRIDLE
HEADPIECE
BROWBAND
THROAT LASH
CHEEKSTRAP
NOSEBAND
BIT
SADDLE
SADDLE PAD
BOOT
STIRRUPS

DRESSAGE ARENA

JUDGE
ENTRANCE
66 YDS. LONG
CENTER LINE
CENTER LETTERS
OUTER MARKERS
22 YDS. WIDE
RAISED BOARDS

DRESSAGE FIGURES

SERPENTINE

CIRCLE

FIGURE EIGHT

VOLTE

NATURAL GAITS

WALK

EACH LEG MUST HIT THE GROUND DISTINCTLY, FOLLOWING A SET SEQUENCE (APPROXIMATELY 4 MPH)

TROT

FRONT AND HIND LEGS AT OPPOSITE SIDES OF THE BODY MUST HIT THE GROUND SIMULTANEOUSLY (APPROXIMATELY 9 MPH)

CANTER

A SLOW GALLOP IN WHICH LEGS HIT THE GROUND IN SEQUENCE, THEN ALL FOUR ARE IN THE AIR SIMULTANEOUSLY (APPROXIMATELY 10-12 MPH)

During a three-day event, horse and rider compete in dressage, *speed and endurance*, and stadium jumping, on consecutive days.

Dressage is worth three points in the total score, speed and endurance 12 and jumping one.

In eventing dressage, the ability of the horse to shorten and lengthen gait is of primary importance.

Speed and endurance is tested over a 4-mile *road and track* run, a 2½-mile *steeplechase* (including 10 obstacles), a longer road and track run and a 5-mile *cross country* run over uneven terrain with numerous obstacles to be jumped.

Stadium jumping includes 10-15 obstacles. Penalty points in each phase are added together and the lowest total score wins.

CROSS COUNTRY

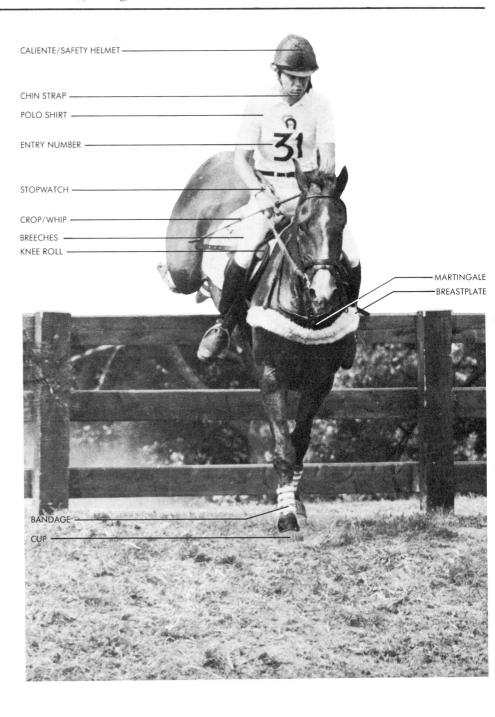

CALIENTE/SAFETY HELMET

CHIN STRAP

POLO SHIRT

ENTRY NUMBER

STOPWATCH

CROP/WHIP

BREECHES

KNEE ROLL

MARTINGALE

BREASTPLATE

BANDAGE

CUP

Two fencers participate in a *match*, *bout* or *assault*, on a narrow mat, strip or piste. They fence with foils, épées or sabres, flexible blunted swords that differ slightly in weight and design.

Before the bout, fencers salute each other, their spectators and a *jury*. The jury director or president orders opponents 'On Guard', asks if they are 'Ready' and commands them to 'Play' or 'Fence.'

Each fencer must wear a chest-protecting plastron under his padded fencing jacket. Women must also wear a breast protector.

EQUIPMENT

SALUTE

FOIL
BLADE
MIDSECTION
FOIBLE
FORTE
BUTTON/TIP/
POINT/END
TONGUE
TRIM
MASK/HELMET
WIRE MESH
BIB
UNDERARM
PROTECTOR
GLOVE
JACKET/
HALF-JACKET
GAUNTLET/
PADDED CUFF
BRANCH/
KNUCKLE BOW
CUISSARD
KNICKERS/
PANTALOONS/
TROUSERS
GROIN STRAP
KNEE HOSE/
SOCKS/
STOCKINGS
FENCING SHOE
PADDING

SECOND POSITION

FIRST POSITION

In foil and saber, fencers who seize the initiative with an *arm extension* or attack receive *fencing precedence* or *right of way* to score. By *deflecting,* or parrying the blade, a defender gets the right of way to *riposte,* or counterattack.

A blade-contacting *engagement* is sought by a fencer who wants to know where the opponent's blade is and how loosely or tightly it is being held. No contact is *absence of blade.*

French is the official judging language of fencing.

STRIP/PISTE/MAT

FOIL & ÉPÉE ELECTRIC SCORING MACHINE/RECORDING MACHINE

SAFETY ZONE/END ZONE/RETREAT ZONE

END LINE/ REAR LIMIT LINE

FOIL WARNING LINE

SABRE & ÉPÉE WARNING LINE

ON-GUARD LINE

CENTER LINE

6'7"

45'11"

ELECTRIC FOIL

9'10"

GUARD SOCKET/ BELL PLUG

FLOOR CABLE

BODY CORD

REEL

3'3"

3'3"

FENCING JACKET

REEL ATTACHMENT

4'11"–6'7"

5'11"–6'7"

SIDELINE

FLÈCHE/ RUNNING ATTACK

ON-GUARD

QUARTE POSITION

PARRY 4

HIGH INSIDE LINE

SEPTIME POSITION

PARRY 7

LOW INSIDE LINE

SIXTE POSITION

PARRY 6

HIGH OUTSIDE LINE

OCTAVE POSITION

PARRY 8

LOW OUTSIDE LINE

Swords are thrust into an opponent's *valid hits*, or valid target areas. Four judges determine the *materiality* of hits in *dry* or *non-electric* matches. The president calls 'Halt' so the jury can reconstruct the *phrase d'armes*, or exchange of blade action. Hits that *land and stick on-target* score points and are called *touches*. Two ground judges referee *electrically scored* matches.

The *bouting* ends when one fencer scores a prescribed number of touches or when a time limit expires: generally five touches or six minutes for men; four touches or five minutes for women. A deciding bout, or *barrage*, is a *fence-off* that settles a tie in foil and sabre. A tie in épée is a defeat for both fencers.

LUNGE

WRIST FLEX
TOUCH/HIT
FOILS
RIGHT-ANGLE FLEX
REAR ARM
THRUST/EXTENSION OF WEAPON ARM
WEAPON HAND
STATIONARY REAR FOOT
ADVANCE LEAD FOOT
LUNGE
ON-GUARD POSITION/BODY BALANCE

FOIL   SABRE   ÉPÉE

TARGET AREAS/VALID HITS AREAS

THRUST & PARRY

PARRY

THRUST

Field hockey is played by two teams of 11 men or women. The object of the game is to use a curved stick to hit a hard leather-covered ball into the opponent's goal. *Goals* may only be scored from within the shooting circle. The team scoring the most goals wins.

The ball may be hit forward, passed, or dribbled, but only with the flat side of the stick. The goalie, except in some penalty situations, may stop the ball with any part of his body, or kick it.

The game is played in two 30-minute halves, with no time-outs except for injury. Play is begun and resumed after a goal, with a two-player face-off called a *'bully,'* at the center of the field.

Violations committed outside the

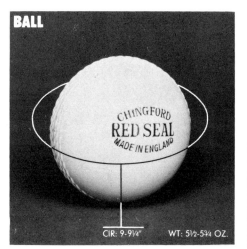

BALL

CHINGFORD
RED SEAL
MADE IN ENGLAND

CIR: 9-9¼"   WT: 5½-5¾ OZ.

FIELD/PITCH

CENTER FLAG   CORNER FLAG

SIDELINE   100 YDS.   5 YD. LINE

LEFT WING
CENTER LINE
GOAL LINE
LEFT INNER
LEFT FULLBACK   LEFT HALFBACK
60 YDS.
GOALKEEPER/GOALIE
GOAL   CENTER HALFBACK   CENTER FORWARD
PENALTY SPOT
RIGHT FULLBACK   RIGHT HALFBACK
SHOOTING CIRCLE/STRIKING CIRCLE   25 YD. LINE   RIGHT INNER

RIGHT WING

shooting circle are penalized by a *free hit*. The defense also receives a free hit if the offense commits a foul inside the circle. If the defense commits an unintentional foul there, the offense receives a *penalty corner*, or free hit from the goal line. Inten-tional fouls within the circle, or unintentional fouls that prevent a sure goal, are penalized by a *penalty stroke* (called a *penalty bully* in women's hockey), taken from the penalty spot.

Violations include '*stick*,' or rais-ing any part of the stick above the shoulder, *obstruction*, *dangerous hitting* (hitting the ball into the air towards a player), *tripping* or *pushing*, or using the rounded side of the stick.

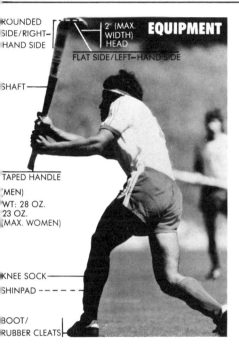

EQUIPMENT

ROUNDED SIDE/RIGHT-HAND SIDE

2" (MAX. WIDTH) HEAD

FLAT SIDE/LEFT-HAND SIDE

SHAFT

TAPED HANDLE (MEN)
WT: 28 OZ.
23 OZ. (MAX. WOMEN)

KNEE SOCK
SHINPAD

BOOT/ RUBBER CLEATS

GOALIE EQUIPMENT

FACE MASK

STEEL TOE
KICKING BOOT/KICKER
ATHLETIC SHOE

CANE FENCING
LEG GUARD

GLOVE

GOAL

CROSSBAR

NET

4 YDS.

GOAL POST

BACKBOARD

SKIRT/KILT

SIDEBOARD (18" HIGH)

GOAL LINE

STICK

FIGURE SKATING
COMPULSORY FIGURES

71

Compulsory, or *school figures,* are worth 30% of total score. All figures are started from a *rest position* and traced three times, one on top of the others. Diameter of the figure should be three times the skater's height. *Loops* must be oval, ⅓-size of circle.

Skaters are judged on distance between *tracings* and other imperfections *(bulge, flatting)* as well as *control, posture, position of hands,* *fingers* and *non-skating foot,* *balance* and overall *grace* and *smoothness.*

All figures are skated on *either forward outside edge* of blade, *backward outside edge, forward inside edge, backward inside edge.*

FIGURE EIGHT/CURVE EIGHT

LONG AXIS

LOBE

SKATING DRESS

SHORT AXIS

FLATTING

TIGHTS

TRACES/TRACING

BULGE

FREE LEG/UNEMPLOYED LEG

SKATING FOOT/EMPLOYED FOOT

ELEMENTS OF COMPULSORY FIGURES/ SCHOOL FIGURES

PARAGRAPH

BRACKET—ONE FOOT HALF-TURN FROM ONE EDGE TO OPPOSITE EDGE, SAME BLADE

THREE—ONE FOOT TURN, FORWARD-BACK OR VICE-VERSA, EITHER EDGE

ROCKER—ONE FOOT TURN, SAME EDGE IN REVERSE DIRECTIONS

THREE

REST POSITION

LOOP—ONE CIRCLE WITHIN ANOTHER, SAME BLADE, SAME EDGE

COUNTER—ONE FOOT TURN SAME EDGE THROUGHOUT

SKATE

BOOT

LACING GAP

HEEL PLATE

STANCHION/BRACE

TOEPICKS/TEETH/NOTCHES

Freestyle, or *free skating*, in both *singles* and *pairs* competition, requires combinations of *spins* and *jumps*, connected by forward and backward *turns*, *spirals*, *lifts* and other maneuvers. Free skating is comprised of a two-minute *short* *program* and a four-or five-minute *long program*, skated to music. The short program includes compulsory moves pre-selected by the judges, while the long program is choreographed by the skater. Both are judged on content, or *artistic im-* *pression*, and skill, or *technical merit*. A perfect score is *6.0*.

Pairs may skate in a *shadowed*, or parallel fashion, or in a *mirror*, or symmetrical manner, but all movements must be synchronized with the music.

AXEL LIFT

IN PAIRS SKATING, LIFTS REQUIRE THE MAN TO PICK HIS FEMALE PARTNER OFF THE ICE. HE MAY NOT USE ANY PART OF HIS BODY EXCEPT HIS HANDS DURING THE LIFT, AND MAY NOT CARRY HER FOR MORE THAN THREE ROTATIONS. A LIFTED SKATER MAY NOT BE TURNED IN A HORIZONTAL POSITION.

DEATH SPIRAL/ BACK OUTSIDE SPIN

IN SINGLES COMPETITION, A SPIRAL IS A SUSTAINED GLIDING MOVEMENT, EITHER FORWARD OR BACKWARDS, USUALLY USED WITH STEPS TO CONNECT JUMPS AND SPINS. IT IS PERFORMED WITH ONE FOOT IN THE AIR. IN PAIRS SKATING, THE DEATH SPIRAL REQUIRES THE MAN TO SPIN IN PLACE WHILE LOWERING HIS PARTNER SO THAT HER HEAD IS INCHES OFF THE ICE.

PARALLEL SPIN/ CAMEL SPIN/ ARABESQUE SPIN

SPINS MUST BE PERFORMED ON ONE SPOT WITHOUT 'DRIFTING.' THEY REQUIRE A MINIMUM OF SIX ROTATIONS OR, IF THERE

IS A FOOT CHANGE, FIVE ON EACH SKATE. IN A GRAB SPIN THE SKATER GRASPS THE FREE SKATE. A SIT SPIN BEGINS AS AN

UPRIGHT SPIN, BUT THE SKATER LOWERS INTO A SITTING POSITION, WITH HIS LEG EXTENDED.

AXEL JUMP

JUMPS ARE DIFFERENTIATED BY THE SKATE EDGE AND BLADE USED TO TAKE OFF AND LAND. SKATERS MAY LEAP OFF EITHER

FOOT, FROM THE EDGE OR TOE OF THE BLADE. ALL JUMPS REQUIRE ONE MID-AIR ROTATION, EXCEPT THE AXEL, WHICH

CONSISTS OF ONE-AND-A-HALF. JUMPS, (EXCEPT THE LUTZ) ARE PERFORMED COUNTER-CLOCKWISE.

Movements and steps in ice dancing are similar to those of ballroom dancing. In competition, couples skate three *compulsory dances*, an original *set dance* and a 4-minute *free skating* program.

Compulsory dances are chosen by lot. Steps, timing and movements must be in accordance with descriptions and diagrams in the international rule book.

Couples may select their own music, tempo, steps and composition for the set dance, but it must be performed to a rhythm named by the international committee.

All steps, turns, changes of position and sequences are permitted in free dancing. Nine judges score each dance, with 6.0 being the highest possible total.

WALTZ HOLD

TANGO HOLD

FOXTROT HOLD

KILIAN HOLD

A football team consists of 11 players. A *game* consists of four 15-minute *quarters*, with a 15-minute break, or *halftime*, between the second and third quarters. A coin toss determines which team *kicks off* to begin play.

The team in possession of the ball, the *offense*, advances it by *running* or *passing*. Action is not continuous. Between *plays* the offense *huddles* to plan the next play. Each attempt to advance the ball is a *down*. If the *defense* prevents the offense from gaining ten yards in four downs it takes control of the ball. If the offense does gain ten yards, it gets a *first down* and an additional four downs to make ten more yards.

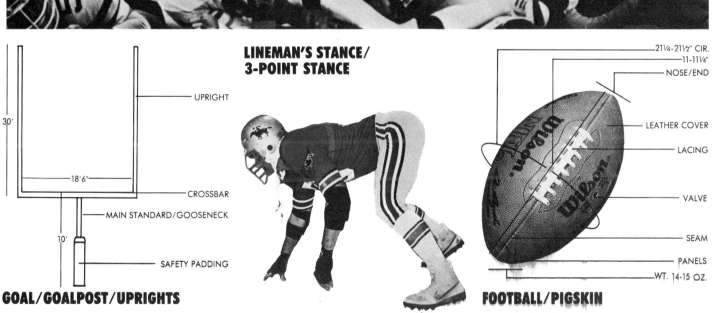

GOAL/GOALPOST/UPRIGHTS

30'

UPRIGHT

18'6"

CROSSBAR

MAIN STANDARD/GOOSENECK

10'

SAFETY PADDING

**LINEMAN'S STANCE/
3-POINT STANCE**

FOOTBALL/PIGSKIN

21¼-21½" CIR.

11-11¼"

NOSE/END

LEATHER COVER

LACING

VALVE

SEAM

PANELS

WT. 14-15 OZ.

If the offense fails to gain ten yards in three downs it usually elects to *punt*, or kick, the ball on *fourth down*, forcing the defense to take control further downfield. When punting, the offense brings in a *special team* called the *punting* team.

Other special teams include the *field-goal team*, *kick-off team*, *punt return team*, *goal-line defensive team*, and *kick-off return team*. Players may be part of special teams as well as *first string* on regular offensive or defensive teams.

Kickoff and punting teams are known as *suicide squads* because of the high degree of injury.

Teams employ numerous offensive and defensive formations based on their skills and the game situation.

FOOTBALL FIELD/GRIDIRON

SIDELINE/OUT-OF-BOUNDS LINE

50-YARD LINE/MIDFIELD

10-YARD LINES

5-YARD LINES

3-YARD CONVERSION LINE (COLLEGE)

2-YARD CONVERSION LINE (PRO)

GOALPOST/UPRIGHTS

INBOUND LINES/HASH MARKS

YARD LINES

END LINE

END ZONE

GOAL LINE

'COFFIN CORNER'

DEFENSIVE FORMATION/'4-3-4'

RIGHT SAFETY/FREE SAFETY/ DEFENSIVE BACK

MIDDLE LINEBACKER/ INSIDE LINEBACKER

RIGHT CORNERBACK/ RIGHT CORNER

RIGHT LINEBACKER/ OUTSIDE LINEBACKER/ WEAK SIDE LINEBACKER

RIGHT DEFENSIVE TACKLE

RIGHT DEFENSIVE END

FOOTBALL

CENTER/'SNAPPER'

SPLIT END/WIDE RECEIVER/ WIDE OUT

LEFT TACKLE/ WEAK SIDE TACKLE/ QUICK TACKLE

LEFT GUARD/ WEAK SIDE GUARD/ QUICK GUARD

HALFBACK/ LEFT HALFBACK/ BALL CARRIER/RUNNING BACK

LEFT SAFETY/STRONG SAFETY/ MONSTER/ROVER

LEFT CORNERBACK/LEFT CORNER

LEFT LINEBACKER/ OUTSIDE LINEBACKER/ STRONG SIDE LINEBACKER

LEFT DEFENSIVE TACKLE

LEFT DEFENSIVE END

RIGHT GUARD/STRONG SIDE GUARD/ TIGHT GUARD

RIGHT TACKLE/STRONG SIDE TACKLE/ TIGHT TACKLE

TIGHT END/BLOCKING END

FLANKER/WIDE OUT/HALFBACK

QUARTERBACK/'FIELD GENERAL'

FULLBACK/RIGHT HALFBACK/ RUNNING BACK/BLOCKING BACK/ BALL CARRIER

◯ OFFENSE   X DEFENSE

OFFENSIVE FORMATION/T FORMATION

POWER I

SHOTGUN

SINGLE WING

BASIC FORMATIONS

COACH'S DIAGRAM/RUNNING PLAY

**FIELD TERMINOLOGY/
'SLANG' FIELD/
AREAS OF PLAY**

A *touchdown*, or *TD*, worth six points, is scored by getting the ball across goal line in an offensive player's possession. The scoring team then attempts a *point-after-touchdown*, or *PAT*, by kicking the ball above the crossbar between the uprights. In some leagues the scoring team may attempt to run or pass the ball over the goal line for a *two-point conversion*.

The offense may also elect to placekick the ball through the goalposts from anyplace on the field. This *field goal* is worth three points.

The defense can score a two-point *safety* by tackling an offensive player with the ball in his own end zone. The team scoring the most points wins.

PASSING FROM THE POCKET

COACHES DIAGRAM/PASSING PLAY

PASS PATTERNS/PASS ROUTES

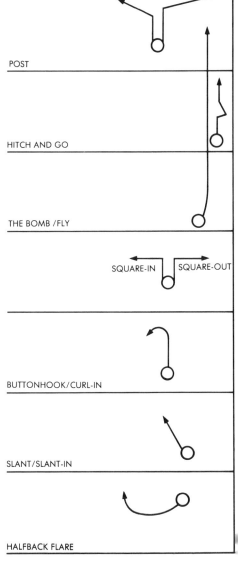

POST

HITCH AND GO

THE BOMB /FLY

SQUARE-IN   SQUARE-OUT

BUTTONHOOK/CURL-IN

SLANT/SLANT-IN

HALFBACK FLARE

FOOTBALL EQUIPMENT

PROTECTIVE PADDING

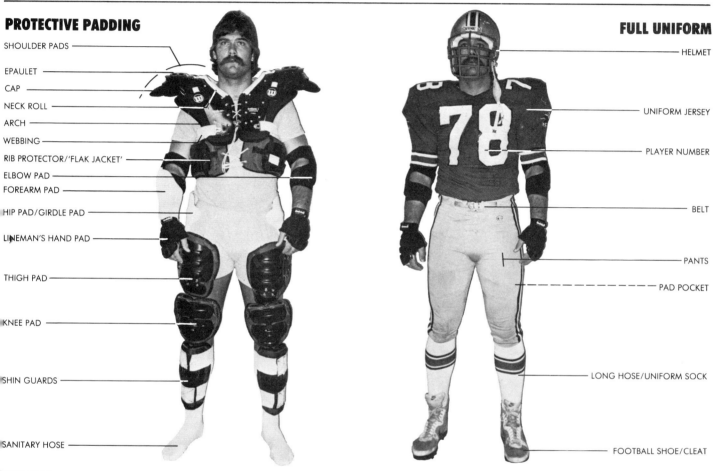

SHOULDER PADS

EPAULET

CAP

NECK ROLL

ARCH

WEBBING

RIB PROTECTOR/'FLAK JACKET'

ELBOW PAD

FOREARM PAD

HIP PAD/GIRDLE PAD

LINEMAN'S HAND PAD

THIGH PAD

KNEE PAD

SHIN GUARDS

SANITARY HOSE

FULL UNIFORM

HELMET

UNIFORM JERSEY

PLAYER NUMBER

BELT

PANTS

PAD POCKET

LONG HOSE/UNIFORM SOCK

FOOTBALL SHOE/CLEAT

HELMET

CROWN STABILIZER

NOSE BUMPER

DUAL PNEUMATIC LINER SYSTEM

CHIN STRAP

STABILIZER BLOCKS

BACK SIZER

FASTENERS

FACE MASK/ CAGE/ BIRDCAGE

FRONT SIZER

SHELL

EARHOLE

JAW PAD

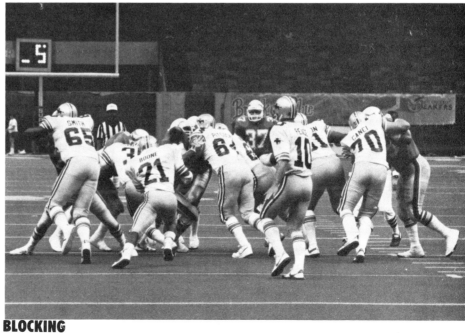

BLOCKING

Officials signal *penalties*, or violations of the rules, by dropping a handkerchief, or *flag*. An *infraction* may be penalized by loss of yards or loss of down, depending on the severity.

In most cases, the unoffending team has the option of accepting the penalty, in which case the official moves the football, or rejecting it and taking the result of the play. Penalty yardage is either added to or subtracted from the *necessary yards*, the yardage needed to gain a first down.

Penalties range from crossing the scrimmage line before the ball is *hiked*, or *snapped*, called *offside*, to more serious penalties such as blocking from behind, or *clipping*.

OFFICIALS' SIGNALS

OFFICIALS' POSITIONING

FIELD JUDGE
UMPIRE
ROD MAN
ALTERNATE
BOX MAN
ROD MAN
CHAIN GANG

SIDE JUDGE
REFEREE
(PUT BALL IN PLAY/
SUPERVISE PENALTIES)
HEAD LINESMAN
(CHAIN GANG SUPERVISOR)
LINE JUDGE/OFFICIAL TIMER
(MARK OUT-OF-BOUNDS)
BACK JUDGE

INTERFERENCE WITH
FORWARD PASS,
FAIR CATCH

INCOMPLETE PASS,
MISSED GOAL,
PENALTY REFUSED

HOLDING

OFFSIDE,
ENCROACHING

ILLEGAL USE OF
HANDS, ARMS, BODY

PERSONAL FOUL;
CLIPPING, ROUGHING

TIME OUT

SAFETY

TOUCHDOWN, FIELD GOAL,
SUCCESSFUL TRY

TRIPPING

FALSE START,
ILLEGAL SHIFT,
ILLEGAL PROCEDURE

INTENTIONAL
GROUNDING OF PASS

DELAY OF GAME,
EXCESS TIME OUT

FIRST
DOWN

ILLEGAL
CRACKBACK

INELIGIBLE RECEIVER,
INELIGIBLE MEMBER OF
KICKING TEAM DOWNFIELD

ILLEGAL CUT, BLOCKING
BELOW THE WAIST

NO TIME OUT, TIME IN WITH WHISTLE

A captain heads a team of 15 players who advance the ball by either kicking it, hitting it with a fist (called *fisting*), or by passing it from player to player. However, no player may carry the ball for more than three steps, and the opposition may tackle or shoulder the carrier.

A game, or *match*, usually lasts for two halves of 30 minutes each, although some championship games have 40-minute halves.

The object is to get the football into the opponent's goal, or *net*. This scores a *goal*, for three points. Getting the ball above the cross-bar and between the goalposts score a *point*, worth one point.

PLAYER

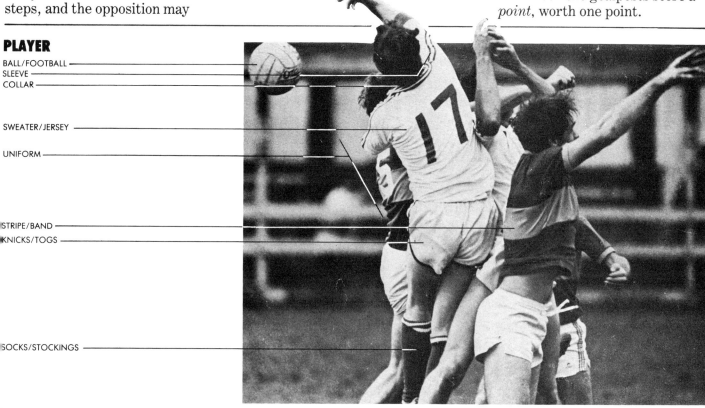

BALL/FOOTBALL
SLEEVE
COLLAR
SWEATER/JERSEY
UNIFORM
STRIPE/BAND
KNICKS/TOGS
SOCKS/STOCKINGS

PITCH/FIELD

GOAL
PARALLELOGRAM
LEFT FRONT FORWARD
CENTER FRONT FORWARD
RIGHT FRONT FORWARD
LEFT HALF FORWARD
CENTER HALF FORWARD
RIGHT HALF FORWARD
LEFT CENTER
RIGHT CENTER
RIGHT HALFBACK
CENTER HALFBACK
LEFT HALFBACK
RIGHT FULLBACK
CENTER FULLBACK
LEFT FULLBACK
GOALTENDER

160 YDS
50-YARD LINE
21-YARD LINE
14-YARD LINE
NET
100 YDS

BALL/FOOTBALL/GAELIC FOOTBALL

PANEL
VALVE
SEWING

WEIGHT: 13–15 OZ.
CIRCUMFERENCE: 27"–29"

A golf course generally consists of 18 holes of widely differing distances and design. The object of the game is for the *golfer*, or *player*, to hit the ball into a cup located on a smooth, grassy area called a green at the end of the hole. Most holes are protected by *hazards*, usually water or sand traps, to make this more difficult. To do this he may select from as many as 14 clubs, each of which has a different function.

Each swing at the ball is a *stroke*. In *medal play*, the golfer completing the course with the lowest stroke total wins. In *match play*, the golfer who takes the fewest strokes on a hole wins that hole, and at the end of 18 holes, or a *round*, the golfer who has won the most holes wins the match.

FAIRWAY

GOLF CART PATH

TEEING AREA
ROUGH/JUNGLE
WATER HAZARD
OUT-OF-BOUNDS

TEEING GROUND

LADIES' TEES/RED TEES

TEE MARKERS

WHITE TEES/
REGULATION
PLAY TEES

GREEN

CHAMPIONSHIP TEES/
BLUE TEES/PROFESSIONAL TEES

GOLF COURSE/LINKS

ROAD
SAND TRAP/BUNKER
OVERHANG/LIP

GREEN

HOLE/CUP
FLAGSTICK/STICK/PIN
APRON/FRINGE/COLLAR/FROGHAIR
PUTTING SURFACE/CARPET

BACKSWING

DOWNSWING

FOLLOW-THROUGH

GOLF SWING

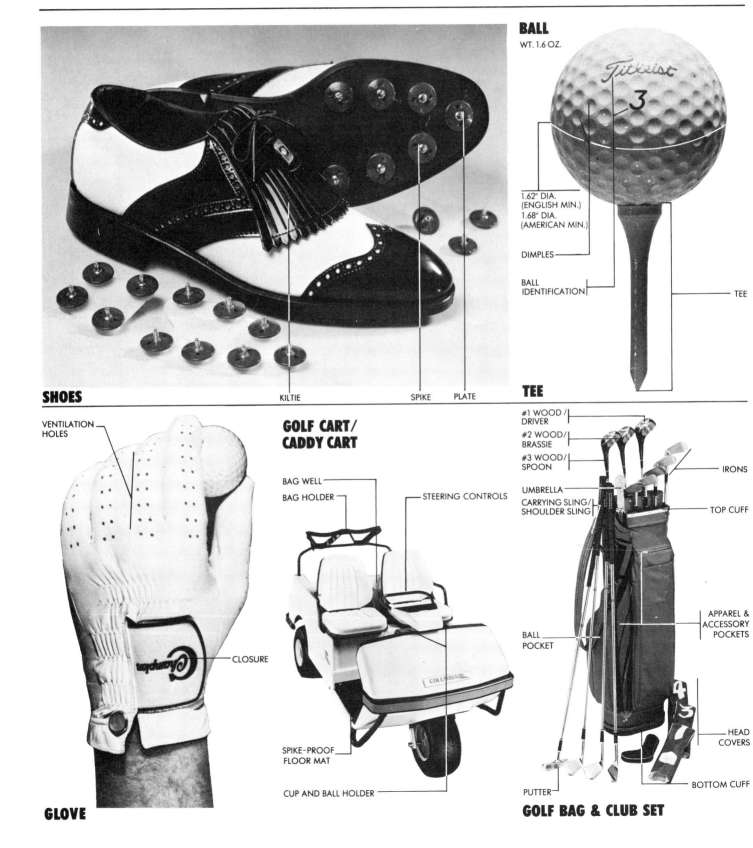

SHOES

KILTIE   SPIKE   PLATE

BALL
WT. 1.6 OZ.

1.62" DIA.
(ENGLISH MIN.)
1.68" DIA.
(AMERICAN MIN.)

DIMPLES

BALL
IDENTIFICATION

TEE

TEE

GLOVE

VENTILATION
HOLES

CLOSURE

**GOLF CART/
CADDY CART**

BAG WELL

BAG HOLDER

STEERING CONTROLS

SPIKE-PROOF
FLOOR MAT

CUP AND BALL HOLDER

#1 WOOD /
DRIVER

#2 WOOD/
BRASSIE

#3 WOOD/
SPOON

IRONS

UMBRELLA

CARRYING SLING/
SHOULDER SLING

TOP CUFF

BALL
POCKET

APPAREL &
ACCESSORY
POCKETS

HEAD
COVERS

PUTTER

BOTTOM CUFF

GOLF BAG & CLUB SET

Clubs are numbered in order of increasing loft, the angle of the club-face to the vertical. A basic club set consists of woods, or drivers, irons used mainly on the fairway, and a flat-faced putter to hit the ball on greens. Golfers may also use spe-cialized clubs, for example a *pitching wedge* or *sand wedge* in certain situations.

The place where a ball stops after being hit is its *lie*. The optimum path between the lie and the hole is called the *line*. Because some fair-ways abruptly change directions, or *dogleg*, and are bordered by *obstructions* and hazards, the line is usually the safest, rather than the shortest, distance from tee to hole.

TOE
CROWN
FACE
FACE INSERT
SWEET SPOT
SCORING /
SCORING LINES
NECK
WHIPPING

HEEL
TOE
SOLE

FERRULE
HOSEL
TOP LINE

WOOD

SHAFT

GRIP

RANGE & LOFT OF CLUBS

MIS–HIT DRIVES

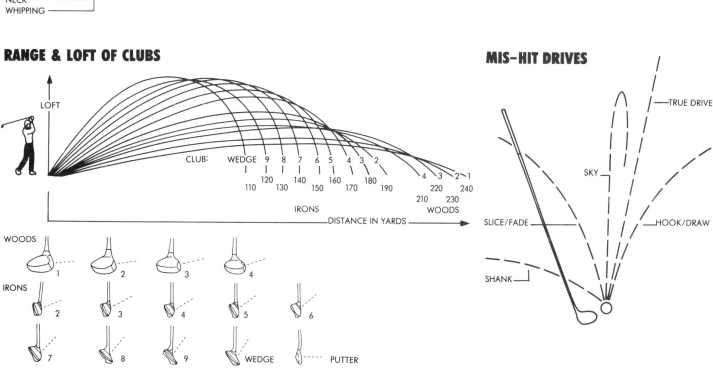

LOFT

CLUB: WEDGE 9 8 7 6 5 4 3 2 1

110 120 130 140 150 160 170 180 190 210 220 230 240

4 3 2 1

IRONS

WOODS

DISTANCE IN YARDS

WOODS
1 2 3 4

IRONS
2 3 4 5 6
7 8 9 WEDGE PUTTER

TRUE DRIVE
SKY
SLICE/FADE
HOOK/DRAW
SHANK

Each hole is designed to be played by an expert golfer in a specific number of strokes, called *par*. Scoring two strokes less than par on a hole is an *eagle*, one stroke less is a *birdie*, one over is a *bogey*, two over is a *double bogey*, three over is a *triple bogey*. *Penalty strokes* are added to the score for rules violations such as kicking a ball.

Inexperienced golfers, known as *duffers* or *hackers*, will often pull their *shot* to their dominant hand causing the ball to hook or draw, or push the ball away from their dominant hand, a slice or fade. Some players even *whiff*, or miss the ball completely. In friendly games they are often given a *mulligan*, or a chance to hit again without penalty.

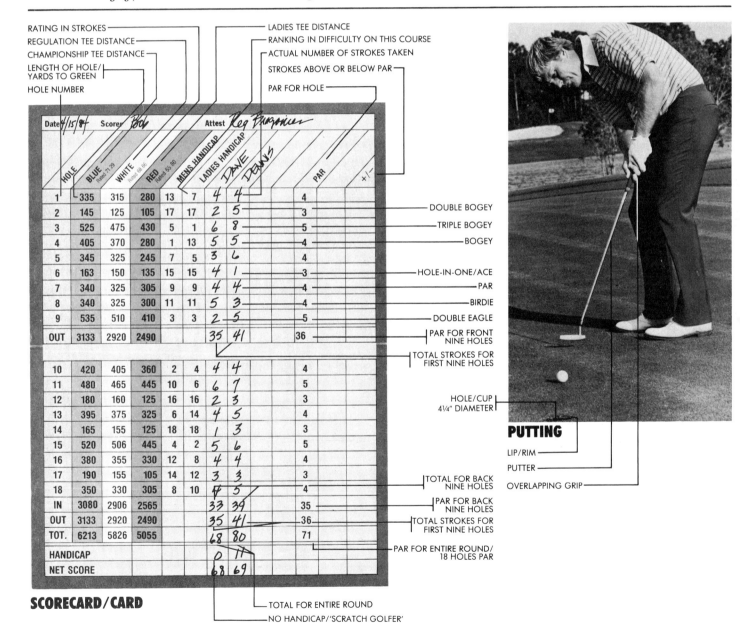

RATING IN STROKES
REGULATION TEE DISTANCE
CHAMPIONSHIP TEE DISTANCE
LENGTH OF HOLE/ YARDS TO GREEN
HOLE NUMBER

LADIES TEE DISTANCE
RANKING IN DIFFICULTY ON THIS COURSE
ACTUAL NUMBER OF STROKES TAKEN
STROKES ABOVE OR BELOW PAR
PAR FOR HOLE

Date 1/15/84	Scorer Bob				Attest Reg Burgoner					PAR	+/-	
HOLE	BLUE Rated 71.29	WHITE Rated 68.66	RED Rated 50.80	MENS HANDICAP	LADIES HANDICAP	JANE	DENNIS					
1	335	315	280	13	7	4	4		4		
2	145	125	105	17	17	2	5		3		DOUBLE BOGEY
3	525	475	430	5	1	6	8		5		TRIPLE BOGEY
4	405	370	280	1	13	5	5		4		BOGEY
5	345	325	245	7	5	3	6		4		
6	163	150	135	15	15	4	1		3		HOLE-IN-ONE/ACE
7	340	325	305	9	9	4	4		4		PAR
8	340	325	300	11	11	5	3		4		BIRDIE
9	535	510	410	3	3	2	5		5		DOUBLE EAGLE
OUT	3133	2920	2490			35	41		36		PAR FOR FRONT NINE HOLES
											TOTAL STROKES FOR FIRST NINE HOLES
10	420	405	360	2	4	4	4		4		
11	480	465	445	10	6	6	7		5		
12	180	160	125	16	16	2	3		3		
13	395	375	325	6	14	4	5		4		
14	165	155	125	18	18	1	3		3		
15	520	506	445	4	2	5	6		5		
16	380	355	330	12	8	4	4		4		
17	190	155	105	14	12	3	3		3		
18	350	330	305	8	10	4	5		4		TOTAL FOR BACK NINE HOLES
IN	3080	2906	2565			33	39		35		PAR FOR BACK NINE HOLES
OUT	3133	2920	2490			35	41		36		TOTAL STROKES FOR FIRST NINE HOLES
TOT.	6213	5826	5055			68	80		71		PAR FOR ENTIRE ROUND/ 18 HOLES PAR
HANDICAP						0	11				
NET SCORE						68	69				

SCORECARD/CARD

TOTAL FOR ENTIRE ROUND
NO HANDICAP/'SCRATCH GOLFER'

PUTTING

HOLE/CUP 4¼" DIAMETER
LIP/RIM
PUTTER
OVERLAPPING GRIP

GYMNASTICS

Gymnastics requires men and women to demonstrate strength, balance, body control and grace on the floor as well as on various pieces of equipment, called *apparatus*.

Men compete in floor exercises, on the vaulting horse, pommel horse, horizontal bars, parallel bars and still rings.

Women compete in floor exercises, the vaulting horse, balance beam, and uneven, or asymmetrical, bars.

In some *meets*, men's and women's trampolining and women's rhythmic events are contested.

Gymnasts may enter one or more events. An *all-around gymnast* competes in all events. *Compulsory* and *optional routines* are performed in each event.

Tumbling, acrobatic movements performed on mats, is the foundation of gymnastics. These movements, and their variations, are incorporated into floor exercises and routines on most pieces of apparatus.

Four judges score each event.

A gymnast's score is determined by eliminating highest and lowest scores and averaging middle ones.

In the compulsory phase, 4 points are given for content and 6 points for execution.

In the optional phase, 6 points are awarded for composition (4 for *difficulty*, 1.5 for *amplitude*, or extension and lift, and .5 for general impression), and four points are given for execution (1.5 amplitude, 1.5 for technical ability and 1 point for impression).

FORWARD ROLL/FRONT PIKE ROLL

BACKWARD ROLL

BACK EXTENSION ROLL

ARABESQUE

HANDSTAND

BACK HANDSPRING

Movements, or *tricks*, are given a difficulty rating by the Federation of International Gymnastics according to the effort required and the risk involved.

To receive the maximum score in this phase, the gymnast must include in his or her routine tricks rated *A parts*, or movements of lower difficulty, *B parts*, tricks of intermediate difficulty, and *C parts*, movements of superior difficulty. The precise number of each part to be included varies according to event.

More difficult parts may be substituted for movements rated less difficult. Gymnasts are penalized for not including the proper number of parts in their routines.

WALKOVER

BACK WALKOVER

BACK WALKOVER SPLIT

CARTWHEEL

SIDE AERIAL

KICKTURN ARABESQUE/SCALE

Floor exercises must be performed within the boundary line, and the gymnast must make use of the whole mat, working in all four corners.

Men have 50 to 70 seconds to complete a routine that emphasizes tumbling skills, but also includes demonstrations of flexibility, strength hold and balance.

Women's exercises last 60 to 90 seconds and are performed to music selected by the gymnast. Women are judged on grace, balance, rhythm, modern and classical dance skills as well as flexibility, tumbling ability, strength and personality.

Rhythmic gymnasts must perform variously with a bouncing ball, a flat, 10½ oz. hoop, two 5¼ oz. balanced *clubs*, a rope, and a flowing colorful *ribbon*.

FLOOR EXERCISE

ROUND-OFF, FLIP FLOP TO 1½ TWISTING 1 ¾ SALTO (SOMERSAULT)

JUMP SIDEWARD TO UNDERCIRCLE RIGHT (LEG) TO LEFT (LEG) SUPPORT, FULL TURN TO STAND

ROUND-OFF, ARABIAN DIVE ROLL

STRADDLE ROLL TO HANDSTAND

REVERSE PIROUETTE

STOOP THROUGH ARMS TO BACK LYING POSITION TO A 'V' SUPPORT (HOLD)

PULL THROUGH TO HANDSTAND ON FINGERTIPS, LOWER LEGS SLOWLY TO STRAIGHT STAND

ROUND-OFF, FLIP FLOP, DOUBLE BACK SALTO

½ TURN AND DROP TO FRONT SUPPORT, PUSH UP CIRCLING LEFT LEG TO REGULAR SPLITS

DOUBLE LEG CIRCLE

'THOMAS FLAIR' STRETCHED UNDERCIRCLES, TO SPLITS

TURN LEFT TO FRONT SUPPORT, SINGLE LEG STOOP UP TO STRETCHED STAND

ROUND-OFF, DOUBLE TWISTING BACK SALTO TO FINAL POSE

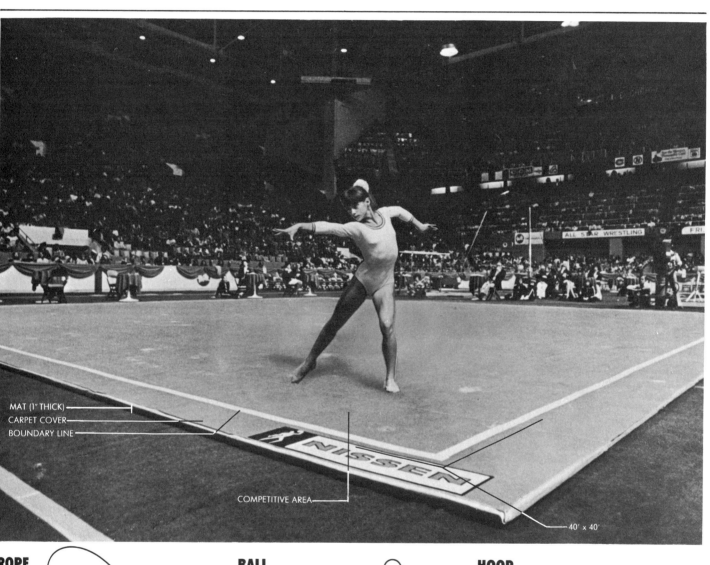

MAT (1" THICK)
CARPET COVER
BOUNDARY LINE

NISSEN

COMPETITIVE AREA

40' x 40'

ROPE

BALL

HOOP

WOMEN'S RHYTHMIC EXERCISE

Men vault over the length of the horse, while women vault over its width. *Vaulters* are permitted two attempts, with only the highest scored vault counting.

There are three types of vaults; *handstand*, *horizontal* and *vaults with turns*. Gymnasts may only touch the horse with their hands. Vaults are judged on *difficulty* (prior to competition judges assign ratings), pre-flight, post-flight and *form and execution*.

During pre-flight, men must be a minimum of 20° above the horizontal top of the horse at repulsion.

Post-flight must be higher than pre-flight.

Women are permitted one step upon landing without penalty, if it is not caused by loss of balance.

SPRINGBOARD/RUETHER BOARD/ BEAT BOARD

3'11"

VAULTING BOARD

STEEL COMPRESSION SPRING

MEN'S VAULT

REPULSION

PRE-FLIGHT/ FIRST FLIGHT

TAKE-OFF

PIKE POSITION

POST-FLIGHT/ SECOND FLIGHT

LANDING

5'4" LONG

4'5" HIGH

WOMEN'S VAULT

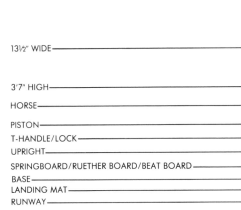

13½" WIDE

3'7" HIGH

HORSE

PISTON

T-HANDLE/LOCK

UPRIGHT

SPRINGBOARD/RUETHER BOARD/BEAT BOARD

BASE

LANDING MAT

RUNWAY

Pommel horse routines require clean swings without stopping. A gymnast will be judged on how often he turns to face a different direction and the number of times he moves up and down the horse, or *travels*.

Basic exercises are undercuts (in which the gymnast releases one hand from the pommel and brings his leg around), circles and scissors. In the optional phase, double leg circles must predominate.

The gymnast is penalized for touching the horse with any part of his body except his hands, for lack of amplitude in double leg circles and for performing scissors below head height.

The gymnast must be *supported* by his hands and arms exclusively.

DOUBLE LEG CIRCLES

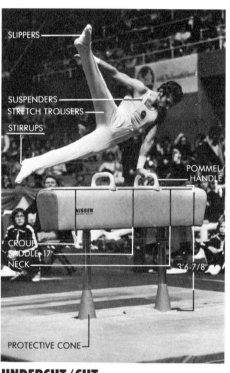

UNDERCUT/CUT

FRONT SCISSORS/LEG WORK

The rings are suspended 8′2″ above the ground and are 19″ apart. The rings must remain still throughout the routine. The gymnast must alternate between swinging parts (movements of his body), hold positions (which must be maintained for 2 seconds), and strength parts.

A routine must include two handstands, one showing strength, the other swung into from below the rings.

A gymnast is penalized for shaking the rings and for unintended movements of his body.

A *giant* is a trick in which the gymnast, starting from a handstand, does a complete circle to return to the handstand.

Somersaults are often used in *dismounting*, or releasing the rings.

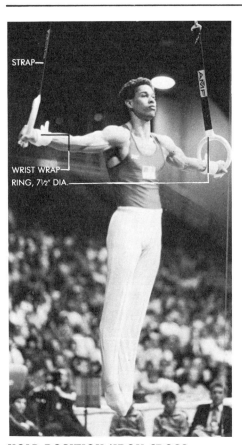

STRAP
WRIST WRAP
RING, 7½″ DIA.

HOLD POSITION/IRON CROSS

STRENGTH MANEUVER/PULLOUT

SWINGING PART/HANDSTAND

Routines on the high bar are composed of a *mount*, giant swings that allow the gymnast to make numerous changes in his grip and direction, and a dismount. The gymnast must swing throughout his entire routine without stopping. To gain maximum score, he must include at least one move in which he releases the bar with both hands simultaneously and regrasps it.

A competitor is penalized for hesitations or for holding a position.

Dismounts often reach heights above 12′ and include twists, flips and somersaults, but all must end with a controlled *landing*.

REVERSE GIANT

DISMOUNT

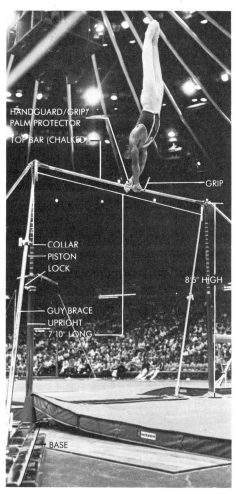

HANDGUARD/GRIP/
PALM PROTECTOR

TOP BAR (CHALKED)

GRIP

COLLAR
PISTON
LOCK

8'5" HIGH

GUY BRACE
UPRIGHT
7'10" LONG

BASE

GRIP CHANGE DURING GIANT SWING

RELEASE AND REGRASP OF BAR

Almost every gymnastic movement can be performed on the parallel bars since the gymnast may use one or both bars, perform between or outside them, or under and over the bars.

A routine on the parallel bars must include both swinging and hold parts. Strength parts are not required, but are allowed.

The gymnast must work smoothly. He is permitted only three pauses of 2 seconds, or *stops*. A move held longer than 3 seconds is penalized. He must release either one or both hands during almost every movement.

Parallel bars may be mounted at either end. A gymnast may use a springboard if a running approach is desired.

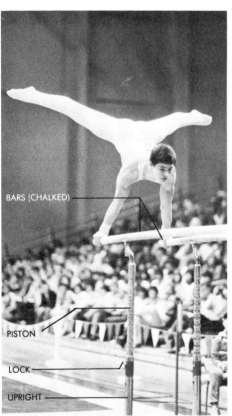

BARS (CHALKED)

PISTON

LOCK

UPRIGHT

**STRENGTH PART/
PRESS TO A HANDSTAND**

11'5" LONG

1'5" WIDE

5'6" HIGH

PARALLEL BARS

ROUTINE

SWINGING PART/
DROP TO UNDERBAR SOMERSAULT

FORWARD PIROUETTE
HOLD/HANDSTAND
SUPPORT·POSITION

MOUNT

CHANGE OF DIRECTION/
'STUTZ'

SWINGING PART
RELEASE/FLIGHT

TUCK POSITION

DISMOUNT/DOUBLE BACK SALTO

The uneven parallel bars are 1'5" apart. A routine consists of a mount, for which a springboard may be used, free flowing swinging movements around both bars (which should include releases, regrasps, changes of direction, kips and twists) and a dismount. Kips, moving from a hanging position below the bar to a support position above the bar, are necessary to maintain continuous motion.

Gymnasts are judged on the passage of the body between the bars, the different hand grips used on each bar, suspension and the composition of the routine.

The routine should be continuous. Two pauses are allowed, but the gymnast may only remain static for a brief period.

GLIDE KIP

CAST WRAP

TOP BAR/RAIL
11'5"
GUY BRACE
7'6"
LOW BAR/RAIL
4'11"
GUY WIRE
SPREADER BAR

CAST WRAP TO DISMOUNT

A routine on the balance beam includes dance moves, acrobatic moves and tumbling moves, all demonstrating the gymnast's balance.

The exercise should be dominated by standing moves, but should include sitting, crouching and lying on the beam, tricks executed in both upright and vertical positions, left and right 180° turns on one foot, leaps and jumps showing good height and distance, and stepping movements, including running steps with dramatic arm configurations.

The gymnast has 70 to 90 seconds to complete her routine, which must continue without hesitation. Three brief *still positions* are permitted.

A gymnast falling off the beam has 10 seconds to resume her routine.

TUMBLING MOVEMENT/CARTWHEEL

BEAM
WORKING SURFACE
(SUEDE COVERED)
4" WIDE
16'3" LONG
3' 11" HIGH

BALANCE BEAM

INVERTED POSITION

UPRIGHT POSITION

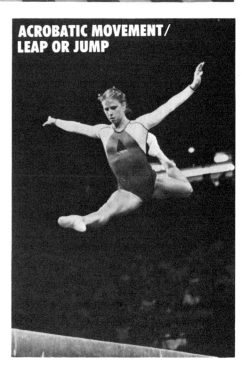

**ACROBATIC MOVEMENT/
LEAP OR JUMP**

Court handball is played by individuals or doubles teams on one-, three- or four-walled courts. Players attempt to hit a *hard rubber* ball so that it bounds off the front wall in such a way that their opponent cannot return it to the front wall on the fly before it bounces twice. A good return, or *volley*, may hit other walls or the ceiling before hitting the front wall.

A game is 21 points. A *match* is two games, with an 11-point *tie-breaker* played if each side wins a game. Only the serving side may score points. A side continues serving until it loses a volley.

Players may hit the ball with any part of one hand. Intentionally blocking, pushing or obstructing is penalized by loss of the volley.

FOUR-WALL COURT
ONE-WALL COURT

FOUR-WALL, SINGLES GAME

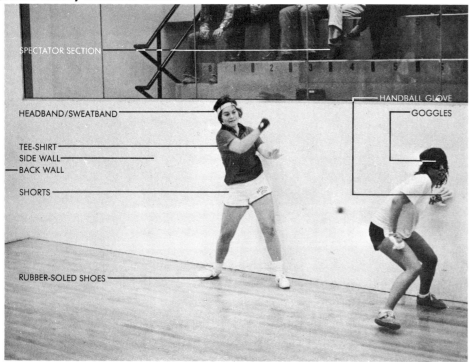

HANDBALL AND HANDBALL GLOVE

ONE-WALL, DOUBLES GAME

Team handball is a non-contact sport played indoors by seven-player teams (as in the Olympics) or outdoors with 11 players. The object is to throw the leather covered ball into the opposition's goal. A game is played in two 30-minute halves.

Players may stop, catch, throw, bounce or hit the ball with any part of their bodies above the knee. They may take only three steps with the ball, then must bounce, or *dribble* it, before taking additional steps. They may hold the ball for three seconds, then must pass, dribble or shoot.

Action centers around the goal area. Only the goalie is allowed inside the area. Shooters can dive into the circle but must throw the ball before touching the ground.

COURT

TOUCHLINE
GOAL LINE
FREE THROW LINE
CENTER LINE
GOAL AREA LINE
PENALTY MARK
GOAL

10'

GOAL AREA/CIRCLE

22 YDS.

6'6"

10'

44 YDS.

BACKCOURT PLAYERS/HALFBACKS
CIRCLE RUNNER/PIVOT PLAYER

GOALKEEPER/GOALIE

23'

WINGS

BASIC ATTACK FORMATION

GOAL AREA/CIRCLE

● -OFFENSE

X -DEFENSE

PENALTY THROW

BALL   WT: 16 OZ. (MEN)
        WT: 13 OZ. (WOMEN)

23" CIR. (MEN)
21½" CIR. (WOMEN)

Thoroughbred horse racing, or *flat racing*, takes place on a level, oval dirt or grass track having no obstacles. Races vary in distance, but are usually a mile or more. Quarter horse races are run on flat tracks over much shorter distances, often a quarter-mile. Both thoroughbred and quarter horses carry a rider, called a jockey.

Harness race horses must pull a driver riding a two-wheeled carriage called a sulky. Harness races are conducted in two gaits (the sequence in which a horse's legs hit the ground), called trotting and pacing.

The first horse and rider, or driver, to cover the race distance without fouling wins.

THOROUGHBRED RACING/FLAT RACING

THOROUGHBRED AND QUARTER HORSE STARTING GATE/"POST"

GATE   STARTING GATE CREWMAN   GATE NUMBER   POLE POSITION   STARTER'S STAND
Ruidoso Downs
TIRE
10 9 8 7 6 5 4 3 2 1
STARTING GATE MOVER
STARTER (WITH ELECTRONIC STARTER B.T. BUTTON)

RACETRACK/RACEWAY/RACECOURSE

7 FURLONG CHUTE/   CLUBHOUSE TURN   OUTSIDE RAIL
7/8 MILE CHUTE   INSIDE RAIL
3/4 POLE   7/8 POLE
5/8 POLE   FINISH LINE/ 'THE WIRE'
BACKSTRETCH   1/16 POLE
TOTE BOARD/ BETTING BOARD
1/2 POLE   HOMESTRETCH
INFIELD   1/8 POLE
3/16 POLE
3/8 POLE   1/4 POLE
TURF COURSE & STEEPLECHASE COURSE   1 1/4 MILE CHUTE
FAR TURN   NURSERY COURSE (3 FURLONGS)

There are many types of races. *Maiden races* are for horses that have never won. In *handicaps*, a *track secretary* assigns a total weight (consisting of jockey, saddle and *lead weights*), to be carried by a horse in an attempt to equalize a *field*. Handicaps are based on past performance. Weights are also assigned in *allowance races*, set according to formula.

All horses in a *claiming race* may be bought for the *claiming price* before a race starts. This prevents horses more valuable than the set price from entering.

Better horses run in *sweeps*, or *sweepstakes*, in which the winner's prize, or *purse*, is made up of owner's entry fees supplemented by money 'put up' by the track.

RACEHORSE/MOUNT & JOCKEY

WHIP/BAT/CROP/STICK
CRASH HELMET/'SKULL CAP'
GOGGLES
STARTING GATE NUMBER/ PROGRAM NUMBER
BLINKERS/BLINDERS/ BLINKER HOOD/ ROGUE'S BADGE
SHADOW ROLL
CROWN PIECE
NECK PIECE — BRIDLE
HEAD PIECE
BIT
REIN

SILKS/COLORS
SADDLE
NUMBER CLOTH
SPUR
BOOT
LEADWEIGHT (HANDICAP WEIGHT)
STIRRUP IRON
LEATHERS/WEBS

BANDAGES

BOOT

GIRTH & SURCINGLE   GIRTH PAD

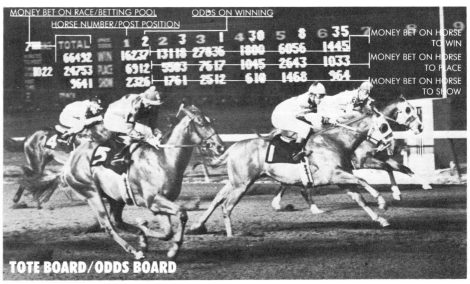

MONEY BET ON RACE/BETTING POOL   ODDS ON WINNING
HORSE NUMBER/POST POSITION
MONEY BET ON HORSE TO WIN
MONEY BET ON HORSE TO PLACE
MONEY BET ON HORSE TO SHOW

TOTE BOARD/ODDS BOARD

Horse racing is a betting sport. *Bettors* wager money on their ability to predict which horses will finish first, second or third, called win, place and show. The *payoff,* the amount of money won, is determined by the *odds.* Odds are the amount of money bet on one horse in relation to the amount bet on the race as a whole.

In *parimutuel betting* the total amount bet is distributed to people holding winning tickets after track operating expenses and state taxes have been deducted.

Exotic bets include the *double,* in which winners of two races are picked, the *quinella,* in which the first two finishers are picked, and the *trifecta,* in which the three finishers are picked in order.

DRIVER IN SULKY/"BIKE" & PACER IN HARNESS

COMBINATION SHOE/ROUND AND SWEDGE SHOE WT:5 OZ.

PARIMUTUEL TICKET/ BETTING TICKET

RACING PROGRAM ENTRY

PAST PERFORMANCE CHART

MOBILE STARTING GATE

TROTTING AND PACING GAITS

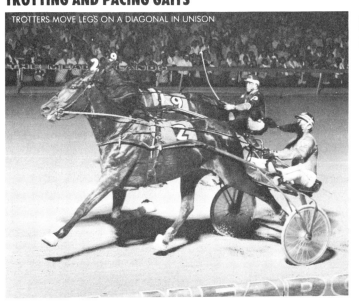

TROTTERS MOVE LEGS ON A DIAGONAL IN UNISON

PACERS MOVE LEGS ON SAME SIDE IN UNISON

FINISH LINE PHOTO/PHOTO FINISH

The object of horseshoe pitching is to toss a shoe so that it rings, or encircles, the metal stake or comes closer to the stake than an opponent's toss. Each *ringer* is worth three points; each shoe closer than an opponent's shoe is worth one point. Shoes score when landing within 6″ of the stake. Singles matches are usually played to 50 points, doubles matches to 21. *Leaners*, or *hobbers*, and shoes actually touching the stake count only as close shoes. Shoes are tossed, or pitched, underhanded. Each pitcher is allotted two tosses in an *inning*.

PITCHING COURT

FOUL LINE   WALKWAY   FOUL LINE   PITCHING BOX/PITCHER'S BOX

40′
50′
STAKE

LEANER/HOBBER

TOE CALK

HEEL CALKS

HORSESHOE/SHOE

STAKE
14″

HORSESHOE/SHOE
MAX. 2½ LB

3½″

7½″

RINGER

Captains head teams of 15 players each. They toss for choice of ends of field. Players move the ball down the field by hitting it with the hurley, by knocking it with their hands while the ball is in the air, or by kicking it.

A game consists of two 30-minute halves, with a maximum interval of 10 minutes between halves, called half time.

Sending the ball into the net is a *goal*, worth three points. Sending it over the crossbar and between the goal posts scores one *point*.

The team scoring the most points wins.

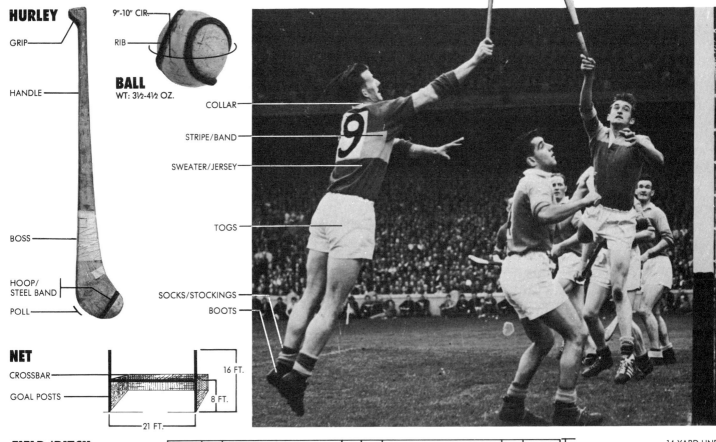

HURLEY

GRIP
HANDLE
BOSS
HOOP/ STEEL BAND
POLL

9"-10" CIR.

BALL
WT: 3½-4½ OZ.

RIB

COLLAR
STRIPE/BAND
SWEATER/JERSEY
TOGS
SOCKS/STOCKINGS
BOOTS

NET

CROSSBAR
GOAL POSTS

16 FT.
8 FT.
21 FT.

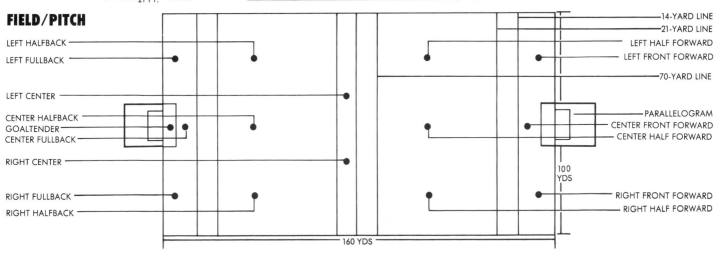

FIELD/PITCH

LEFT HALFBACK
LEFT FULLBACK
LEFT CENTER
CENTER HALFBACK
GOALTENDER
CENTER FULLBACK
RIGHT CENTER
RIGHT FULLBACK
RIGHT HALFBACK

14-YARD LINE
21-YARD LINE
LEFT HALF FORWARD
LEFT FRONT FORWARD
70-YARD LINE
PARALLELOGRAM
CENTER FRONT FORWARD
CENTER HALF FORWARD
RIGHT FRONT FORWARD
RIGHT HALF FORWARD

100 YDS

160 YDS

Iceboating, or *hardwater sailing*, takes place in one- or two-man boats, in classes ranging from nine to 30 feet in length.

Most classes race *windward-leeward* courses which they complete three to five times, circling a pair of marks placed one mile apart.

Before a race, skippers draw for positions, either a *starboard tack position* or a *port tack position*, and wait for a dropped flag. At the start, skippers push their iceboats off and jump into the cockpit.

Most iceboats are made of steel, aluminum or wood, and travel at upwards of 100 miles per hour.

ICEBOAT

HEADBOARD
BATTEN
CLASS SYMBOL
SAIL PANEL
CLUB SYMBOL
SHROUD
BOAT NUMBER
MASTSTEP
GOOSENECK
SAILMAKER'S LOGO
MAINSHEET BLOCKS
SKIPPER
RUNNER PLANK
BOAT NAME
HULL/FUSELAGE
SPRING BOARD
STEERING RUNNER

MAST
FORESTAY

485

WHISPER II

SAIL
WINDOW
SAFETY HELMET/
CRASH HELMET
SAFETY GOGGLES
BOOM
FOUL WEATHER GEAR
SHROUD/SIDESTAY
RUNNER PLANK
RUNNER CHOCK
RUNNER
HULL
MAST
MAIN SHEET
SPIKES/CREEPERS
TILLER
MAINSHEET BLOCK

ICEBOATER

WINDWARD MARK
WIND DIRECTION

LEEWARD MARK
FINISH LINE

COURSE

An ice hockey game consists of three, twenty-minute *periods*.

Rules infractions, or *penalties*, result in the offending player being removed from play, for usually two or five minutes. His team plays *short-handed*, giving the opposition a *power play*.

An offensive player tries to block the goalie's view, or *screen* him. The goalie is credited with a *save* when he knocks a *shot* away. A blinking *red light* atop the goal judge's box is lit when a *goal* is scored.

The angle between the shaft of a stick and the blade is the *lie*. The puck is made of vulcanized rubber. In professional hockey a *sudden-death overtime* (first goal, wins) is sometimes used to decide a game tied at the end of *regulation play*.

RINK

KICK PLATE
SIDEBOARDS/
BOARDS

REFEREE'S CREASE
PLAYER BENCHES

GOAL JUDGE BOX
BACKBOARDS
GOAL/NET
GOAL LINE

60'

NEUTRAL ZONE

SLOT

CENTER CIRCLE

30'

FACE-OFF SPOTS
PENALTY BOX/'SIN BIN'
TIMEKEEPER AND SCORER'S BOX

CENTER LINE/RED LINE
BLUE LINE/ZONE MARKING

FACE-OFF CIRCLE—15' RADIUS
GOAL CREASE
GLASS
DASHER

LINING
TENDON GUARD
TONGUE
COLLAR
UPPER PANEL
LOWER PANEL
HEEL CAP
MANUFACTURER'S LOGO
SOLE
BOOT
HOUSING
BLADE/RUNNER
FLAT EDGE

EYELET
EYELET FACING
LACE
AGLET
TONGUE ATTACHMENT
TOE CAP
POINT

3"

WT. 5½ -6 OZ.

HOCKEY SKATE

PUCK

Physical contact occurs when a player blocks his opponent with his body, or *bodychecks* him. A check may send a player crashing into the *boards*. Trying to steal the puck with a stick is *stick-checking*.

GOAL AND GOALIE/GOALKEEPER/GOALER

HELMET/HEADGEAR

CHIN STRAP
SHOULDER PADS
LACES
ELBOW PAD

HELMET
FACE MASK
SHOULDER AND ARM PROTECTION
CROSSBAR

HIP PAD

GOAL POST
NET
BODY PAD/
CHEST PROTECTOR

PANTS
GLOVE
BACKROLL
PROTECTOR

KNEE PAD

CUFF
WRIST PAD
PALM
POCKET
LACING

CATCH GLOVE

STICK GLOVE
BACKPAD

SHIN PAD/
SHIN GUARD
SOCK

GOAL PAD

GOAL LINE
SHAFT (MAX. LENGTH 58")
SKATE

BOOT
BLADE

SKATE

GOALIE STICK

BLADE
(MAX. WIDTH 3½"/MAX. LENGTH 15½")

BLADE
(MAX. LENGTH 12½")
HEEL
FACE (TAPED)

STICK

PLAYER/CENTER/WING/DEFENSEMAN

PLAYER POSITIONS

LEFT DEFENSEMAN

RIGHT DEFENSEMAN

LEFT WING

RIGHT WING

GOALIE   X

CENTER   X   O   CENTER

GOALIE   O

RIGHT WING

LEFT WING

RIGHT DEFENSEMAN

LEFT DEFENSEMAN

OFFICIALS SIGNALS

HIGH-STICKING	CROSS-CHECKING	DELAYED CALLING OF PENALTY	HOLDING	HOOKING	INTERFERENCE
WASH-OUT	UNSPORTSMANLIKE CONDUCT	BOARDING	CHARGING	ELBOWING	
MISCONDUCT	ROUGHING	SLASHING	SPEARING	TRIPPING	ICING

SCREEN PLAY

POWER PLAY

BASIC PLAYS

BROKEN LINE INDICATES PUCK MOVEMENT

Herb Brooks
U.S.
Olympic
Team
1980

HERB BROOKS, 1980 GOLD MEDAL
WINNING U.S. OLYMPIC TEAM

Jai alai is played in a *fronton*, an auditorium that includes a court, tiered spectator seating area and *parimutuel betting* facilities. Spectators watch the game through a *mesh screen*.

Jai alai is played by individuals, or two- and three-man teams. The pelota is thrown off the frontis and must be caught in the cesta on the fly or after one bounce, then returned to the wall in a continuous motion.

Only the serving team can score.

The losing team returns to the bench and is replaced by another team. The game ends when a player or team scores enough points to win the match, usually between 6 (singles) and 40. Spectators wager on the results.

SCOREBOARD/ BETTING BOARD

BETTING ODDS FOR NEXT GAME

QUINIELA ODDS

GAME NUMBER

TIME OF DAY

POINTS

POSITION AND ODDS

WIN, PLACE AND SHOW PAYOFF PRICES

BETTING PAYOFFS

CANCHA/COURT

FRONTIS/FRONT WALL

CUSHION/FAULT LINE

LATERAL/SIDE WALL

OUT OF BOUNDS AREA

UNDERSERVE LINE/
FAULT LINE

POSITION LINES

REBOTE/
BACK WALL

40'

176'

40'

10'

PLAYERS' CAGE

THE 'WOOD'

SERVICE LINE

JUDGE

SERVICE AREA

OVERSERVE LINE/
PASS LINE

SERVING PLAYER'S LINE

CESTA/BASKET

GUANTE/GLOVE

COSTILLAS/RIBS

2'

TACO

CINTA

ARO/FRAME

PUNTA/POINT

HELMET

PELOTA/BALL (2" DIA./WT: 4½ OZ.)

FONDO

TEAM NUMBER/POST POSITION

FAJA/SASH

TROUSERS

RUBBER-SOLED SHOES

Karters race miniature race cars, or *karts*, in events conducted to scale with sports car and stock car racing. *Sprint* karters sit upright beside or in front of a 2- or 4-cycle motor and race on a twisting road course consisting of about nine *left-*, *right-* and *ess-turns*. *Speedway* karters, also using 2- or 4-cycle *engines*, run short lap races, or *heats*, around ⅛-mile oval dirt tracks, or *'bullrings.'*

Powerful *roadracing* karts are driven in a reclining, or *'laydown position'*, at speeds of up to 140-mph on full-sized road courses during hour-long *enduro* races. The aerodynamics of some of these *superkarts* are similar to full-sized race cars, enabling karters to create *drafts* and *slipstreams.*

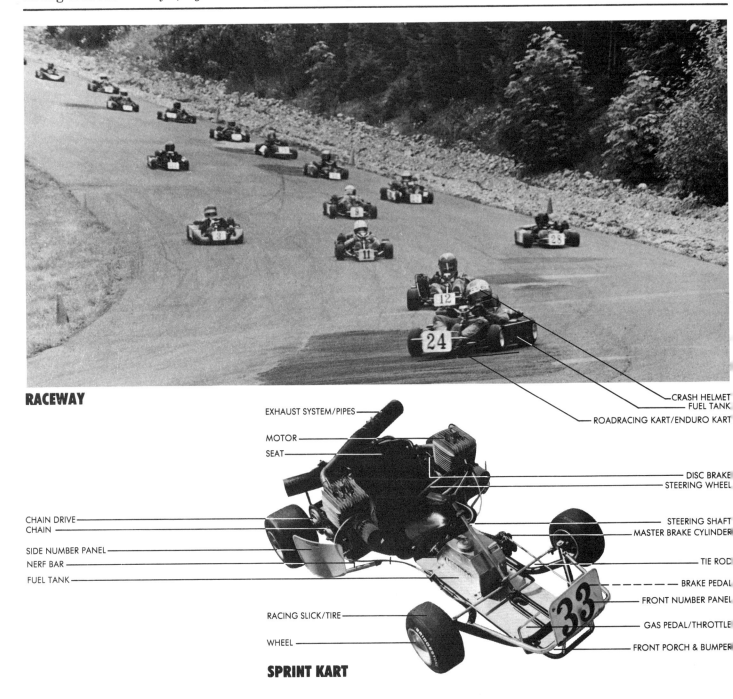

RACEWAY

CRASH HELMET
FUEL TANK
ROADRACING KART/ENDURO KART

EXHAUST SYSTEM/PIPES
MOTOR
SEAT

DISC BRAKE
STEERING WHEEL

CHAIN DRIVE
CHAIN
SIDE NUMBER PANEL
NERF BAR
FUEL TANK

STEERING SHAFT
MASTER BRAKE CYLINDER

TIE ROD
BRAKE PEDAL
FRONT NUMBER PANEL

RACING SLICK/TIRE
GAS PEDAL/THROTTLE

WHEEL
FRONT PORCH & BUMPER

SPRINT KART

A men's team is made up of 10 players, and games consist of four 15-minute *quarters*, with two-minute rest intervals between the first and third quarters and a 10-minute break, or *half time*, after the second quarter.

Women's teams are made up of 12 players, and their games consist of two 25-minute halves, with a 10-minute half-time.

The two *center players* engage in a *face-off* at the center line to begin a game. All players must then stay in their assigned areas throughout play.

The ball is carried, thrown and caught with sticks. Each goal counts one point and the team scoring the most points wins the game.

ATTACKMEN
WING AREA
MIDFIELDERS

GOAL AREA

NET (6 FT.)
END LINE

GOALTENDER/GOALIE

DEFENSEMEN

MIDFIELD LINE/CENTER LINE

15 YDS.

10 YDS.

110 YDS.

53⅓-60 YDS.

FIELD

SPECIAL SUBSTITUTION AREA
SIDELINE

OFFSIDES   SLASHING   HOLDING   PUSHING   FACE-OFF

REFEREE SIGNALS

SCOOP
POCKET
BALL
STOP

KNOB / BUTT END/BUTT
SHAFT
THROAT
SIDEWALL
MESH
HEAD
TOP LIP

STICK

FINGERS

SEGMENTED THUMB

PALM

WRISTPAD

SUPPORT LACING

GLOVE

NET

BIB
STICK
CHEST & STOMACH PAD

GOAL
BALL

HELMET
FACE MASK/MASK
CHIN STRAP
CHIN PAD
SHOULDER PAD
ELBOW PAD
FLOATING CUFF
GLOVE

JERSEY

SHORTS/TRUNKS/PANTS

LAWN BOWLING

Lawn bowling, also called *bowls* or *flat green bowls*, is played on a green which is divided into *rinks*. Matches are played by individuals or teams. A toss determines who bowls first. The mat, or footer, is placed and the jack is delivered.

While standing on the mat *bowlers* roll their bowls next to the jack, maybe even getting a *toucher*.

A point is awarded for each bowl closer to the jack than the opposi-tion's nearest bowl. After all bowls are rolled, a new *end* is begun.

Matches may be played either for a certain number of ends or to a predetermined number of points.

RINK NUMBER

DITCH/WALL

MAT/FOOTER

CENTER OF RINK MARKER

GREEN/BOWLING GREEN

SCORER

CALIBRATED TAPE/TAPE

LOCATING SPIGOT

TAPE HANDLING

CALIPERS

MEASURE

JACK/KITTY

EMBLEM/ENGRAVING

BOWL/WOOD

BOWLS & JACK

International *lugers* race in iced *courses* having at least one *labyrinth, straightaway,* and *left-, right-, hairpin-,* and *S-curve.* The *starting line* is crossed in a *flying start,* usually from raised *starting blocks.* Racers *'flow in the ice groove.'* They find their *driving track,* the shortest path from start to finish. Lugers lean backward to reduce *air resistance;* stamp on *sled runners,* pull *reins* and shift weight to *steer;* and *brake* by pressing their soles against the ice while pulling the front of the *luge* into the air. *Double-seaters* have a *sunken seat* for the second rider who lies under the first while *luging.* Aggregate times from a series of *runs* determine winners. Courses are about 1000 meters long.

LUGER/LUGE TOBOGGANIST/LUGE RACER
PLASTIC-COATED RACING SUIT
KNEE PROTECTOR
PADDED GLOVE
GLOVE STUDS
START HANDLE
LUGE TOBOGGAN SLED/LUGE/RODEL

CRASH HELMET
FACE SHIELD/VISOR
ELBOW GUARD
MANUFACTURER'S LOGO
SUPPORT BELT/KIDNEY PROTECTION BELT
BOOTIES/BOOTS/SHOES
FRONT BRIDGE
RUNNER/BLADE/ 'STEELS'
RUNNER

THE START

LUGE TOBOGGAN SLED/ LUGE/RODEL

ARC/ 'ROCKER'
STABILIZER
RUNNER BLADE/ 'STEELS'
BOLT/RIVET
RUNNER
SEAT FASTENING/CLASPS
'BOX'
SEAT BOLT
FRONT BRIDGE
LEATHER STRAP
SEAT

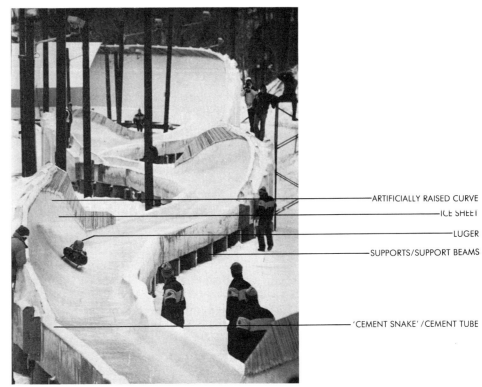

ARTIFICIALLY RAISED CURVE
ICE SHEET
LUGER
SUPPORTS/SUPPORT BEAMS
'CEMENT SNAKE' /CEMENT TUBE

LUGE/TRACK/COURSE/RUN

There are over 50 types of martial arts, with variations and individual styles within each type. Competitive tournaments, sanctioned by organizational bodies and international committees, exist for several of the martial arts. However, since many of the *fighting arts* develop spiritual skills as well as self-defense techniques, much of the sport is more concerned with private activity than with public competition.

Martial arts practitioners work out in a dojo, or school, run by a *sensei*, a master or teacher.

The *double middle quarter block in horse stance* shown below illustrates the fluid movement, strength and quickness typical of martial arts moves.

Karate, or *empty-handed fighting*, is characterized by crippling kicks and punches meant to disable an attacker or group of attackers. Participants, or *players*, engage in two types of sanctioned matches: *kata* (form) and *kumite* (sparring).

In kata, a formal exercise in which an individual performs various movements according to a prescribed pattern, contestants are judged on form, appropriate speed and strength, and on correct breathing and direction of movement. The action, which simulates simultaneous combat with a number of attackers from several directions, is judged on a scale of zero to ten. The player with the most points wins.

KATAS

BACK-STANCE KNIFE HAND   HEEL FRONT KICK

SHOULDER-WIDTH STANCE   REVERSE RIGHT-HAND PUNCH   REVERSE LEFT-HAND

KUMITES

ATTACK BY MALE   AVOIDANCE BY FEMALE   ARM LOCK BY FEM

LUNGE PUNCH BY MALE   BLOCK DEFLECTED BY FEMALE

n kumite matches, a player directs kicks and punches at his opponent while also blocking his opponent's attacks. Physical contact is strictly limited, thus blows need not actually land to score and are pulled back at the last moment to avoid injuring an opponent.

A full point, or *ippon*, is awarded for a likely hit. A less effective blow is awarded a half-point, or *waza ari*.

Players accumulating a set number of points, or scoring a killing blow, win. A killing blow is one that would have landed in one of the 20 vital points of the body and would have killed the opponent if it had not been pulled back in time.

ROUNDHOUSE KICK   KNIFE HAND

FRONT KICK   CROSS-STEP   SIDE KICK

KNIFE HAND TO BACK OF NECK   FOLLOW THROUGH & RECOVERY

E PUNCH BY FEMALE   STEP & RIDGE HAND TO THROAT   FOLLOW THROUGH

Points in kumite are awarded for blows struck with good form, good attitude, strong vigor, proper timing, an alert mind, or *zanshin*, and correct distancing, within two inches of the target area. A blow that is thwarted or falls short of the correct distance is awarded no score.

Certain karate techniques are not allowed in competition because of their lethal nature. Others, such as dangerous blows to the eyes or testicles, persistent attacks on the shins or direct attacks to the hips, knee joints or insteps, may result in fouls. A player may be disqualified due to repeated fouls after being warned, first privately, then publicly, by the match referee.

BLOCKING A KICK

BLOCKING A PUNCH

FRONT KICK

SIDE KICK

SCORING AN IPPON

NO SCORE

Judo, an Oriental form of wrestling derived from *jujitsu*, or *jujutsu*, its medieval predecessor, combines balance and strength with holding and throwing techniques.

A judo player, or *judoka*, can win a match with an ippon by bodily dumping his opponent on his back, pinning him to the mat and keeping him there for 30 seconds, or by applying a submission hold (such as a twisting lock on the arm or elbow, or a choke hold) until his opponent signifies defeat by *tapping out*, hitting the mat or his attacker twice with the hand. A player is awarded a half-point waza-ari for an imperfect throw. Two waza-aris equal one ippon. A sanctioned match lasts from three to 10 minutes.

DOJO/SCHOOL

UNIFORM/ GI/JUDOGI
BELT/OBI
JACKET/UWAGI
PANTS/ZUBAN
MAT/TATAMI

STRANGLEHOLD

ONE-POINT SHOULDER THROW/IPPON SEOINAGE

JUDO MAT/COMPETITION MAT

52½'

52½'

CONTEST AREA/SHIAIGO (26⅓')
SAFETY AREA
DANGER AREA (3⅓')

Aikido's method of self-defense is based on dodging an attacker while simultaneously using the force of his momentum against him.

Competitive fighting takes various forms. In kata, two participants, one designated attacker, or *uke*, the other defender, or *tori*, are judged on a set routine of attack and defense.

In three-round *ninin dori*, three *aikidoists* stage a spontaneous mock fight. *Tanto randori* consists of two one-minute rounds of free fighting between an unarmed defender and an attacker armed with a rubber knife. The attacker makes a point by striking the defender in the chest with the knife. The defender is awarded a point for disarming his opponent.

WRISTLOCK

WRIST & NECK LOCK

ELBOW LOCK

MAT

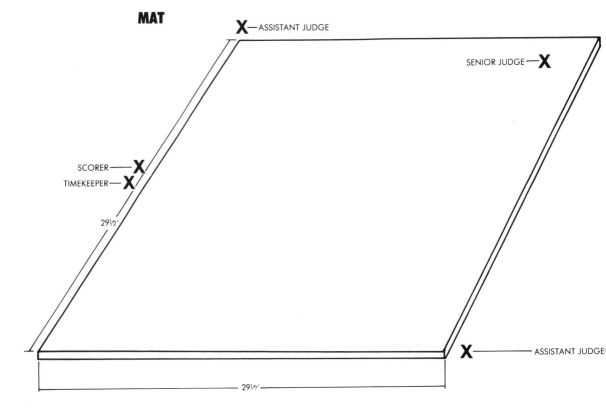

X—ASSISTANT JUDGE

SENIOR JUDGE—X

SCORER—X

TIMEKEEPER—X

29½'

X——ASSISTANT JUDGE

29½'

Kung fu, the Chinese art of self-defense from which karate was developed, is a broad term used to refer to any of a number of martially inspired systems for fighting, fitness and dance.

There are several hundred styles, many of which involve weapons. Other styles use animal postures as spiritual and physical models. Such stances and movements imitate those of a crane, tiger, snake, monkey, etc. The sport also involves free fighting, or *sparring*, in which a variety of styles are used.

Kung fu, called *kempo*, or *wu shu* in China, means "skill" or "ability." Today the emphasis of most forms of kung fu is on its use in combat.

FREE FIGHTING

MONKEY STANCE

CRANE STANCE

When the martial arts are used for fighting, there are certain parts of the body which are more vulnerable to blows than others.

When attacking the head and neck, for example, an open or closed fist, the elbow and the foot are most effective. The eyes, temples and throat are especially vulnerable.

On the other hand, when attacking the groin, body and internal organs, an open or closed fist, the elbow, knee and foot are used with

CLOSED FIST METHODS

INNER WRIST
INNER FOREARM
SKULL
TEMPLE
JAW
CLAVICLE
ARMPIT
SOLAR PLEXUS
ABDOMEN
SHIN
INSTEP

BRIDGE OF NOSE
PHILTRUM
CHIN
ADAM'S APPLE
SIDE OF NECK
WINDPIPE
RIBS
GROIN
SIDE OF KNEE

INSIDE & OUTSIDE ELBOW
BASE OF CEREBELLUM
UPPER BACK
KIDNEY
SMALL OF BACK
COCCYX
VASTUS EXTERNAS
HOLLOW OF KNEE
CALF
ACHILLES TENDON

FORE FIST
BACK FIST
BOTTOM FIST
ONE-KNUCKLE FIST
MIDDLE-FINGER ONE-KNUCKLE FIST
FOREKNUCKLE FIST

greatest effect. Most vulnerable areas are the groin, coccyx, solar plexus and kidney.

When attacking the legs and feet, the foot is used with particular effect against the knee, arch and achilles tendon.

OPEN HAND METHODS

RIDGE HAND

KNIFE HAND

BACK HAND

SPEAR HAND

BEAR HAND

PALM HEEL

TIGER-MOUTH HAND

TWO-FINGER SPEAR HAND

OX-JAW HAND

ELBOW

ONE-FINGER SPEAR HAND

FOOT METHODS

HEEL

BALL OF FOOT

FOOT EDGE

SOLE

INSTEP

KNEE

The martial art of kendo, developed from *kenjutsu*, "the art of the sword," is the Japanese form of fencing with bamboo swords.

In competition, two *kendoka* "cut" with the forward third of their sword or "thrust" with its tip, scoring points by striking either the temples, wrists, breastplate or throat of their opponent. A strike counts as a point only if it is delivered with full spirit and correct form, and is accompanied by a forceful yell, or *kiai*. The first to score two points or the one with the higher score by the time limit, wins.

A kendo match is conducted within a 33- by 36-foot competition area and normally lasts three to five minutes.

SHOMEN STRIKE

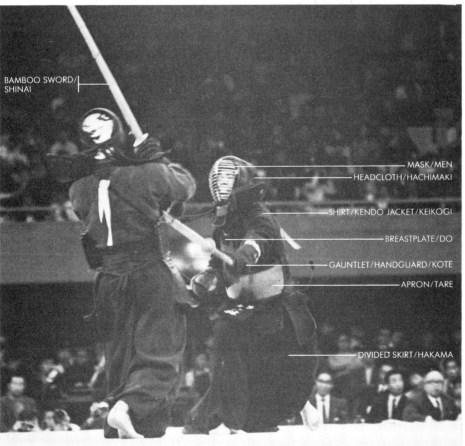

BAMBOO SWORD/
SHINAI

MASK/MEN
HEADCLOTH/HACHIMAKI

SHIRT/KENDO JACKET/KEIKOGI

BREASTPLATE/DO

GAUNTLET/HANDGUARD/KOTE

APRON/TARE

DIVIDED SKIRT/HAKAMA

Motorcycles are raced on many different surfaces which test the *bike's* speed and durability, as well as the rider's skill and endurance. Events include roadracing on a specially built *circuit* or public road; motocross, or *MX*, or *scramble*, which takes place on natural terrain courses with hills, jumps, mud, and other obstacles that require gear changing; *hill climbing*, races against time or distance up a prepared steep hill; *dirt track* racing on an oval track with flat or banked

MOTOCROSS BIKE

THROTTLE CABLE

BRAKE

THROTTLE

FUEL TANK

AIR FILTER

NUMBER PLATE

EXHAUST PIPE

CLUTCH CABLE

AIR SCOOP

RADIATOR

FORK TUBE

CLUTCH

FENDER

BRAKE LINE

TENSION BAR

SPROCKET

SWING ARM

CHAIN

SUSPENSION AIR TANK

KICK STARTER

REAR BRAKE LEVER

CLUTCH COVER

CARBURETOR

MUFFLER

SPOKES

HUB

DISC BRAKE

NOBBY TIRE

OFFICIAL'S STAND

JUMP

SAND WHOOPS

surfaces; and *speedway* races *(handicap, scratch* or *match)*, run on an ash or shale oval track. Dirt track racing requires a special riding technique since these *machines* do not have brakes.

Courses vary in distance and com-

position (from deserts to ice, on which bikers use steel-studded rear tires). Races are conducted in classes determined by the size of bike engines, measured in cubic centimeters (cc's), ranging from lightweight *50cc's* to *unlimited class*

750 + cc's.

Motocross races usually consist of two or three *motos*, or *heats*. They may be held over a set distance, ranging from one to two miles, include a specific number of laps, or simply be determined by distance

ROADRACING BIKE/STREET BIKE

MIRROR
INSTRUMENT CLUSTER
THROTTLE
OVERHEAD CAM
CARBURETOR
FUEL TANK
SISSY BAR
HEADLIGHT
TAIL LIGHT
SEAT
HYDRAULIC BRAKE LINE
SPEEDOMETER CABLE
FRONT FENDER
REAR SHOCK ABSORBER/ BOINGER
REAR SINGLE-DISC BRAKE
RIGHT SIDE COVER
SWING ARM BOLT
REAR BRAKE LEVER
ELECTRONIC POINT COVER
EXHAUST PIPE
FRONT DOUBLE-DISC BRAKES
STREET TIRE

FUEL GAUGE
SPEEDOMETER
TURNING LIGHT
TACHOMETER
RESET BUTTON
INSTRUMENT PANEL
MIRROR
HANDBRAKE
LIGHT SWITCH
CLUTCH
THROTTLE
TURN SIGNAL
HAZARD LIGHTS
FUEL TANK LOCK

CONSOLE

covered in a set length of time. They are generally raced in single bikes, although races with *sidecars* are popular in Europe.

Riders win classification points toward a national championship, as well as prize money.

HELMET

RIDER NUMBER

SUN VISOR

GOGGLES

AIR FILTER

JERSEY

SPONSOR'S DECALS

PADDED GLOVES

PADDED PANTS

KNEE CUPS

SHIN GUARDS

BOOTS

MOTOCROSS RIDER

MOTOCROSS TRACK

WHOOPS

PIT, JUMP, PIT

JUMP

START GATE

MOUNDS

JUMPS

PIT

JUMP

SAND WHOOPS

CAMEL BACK RAMP

4' HIGH JUMP

Cross-country *orienteers* use protractor compasses and topographic maps, or specially drawn orienteering maps in a race to reach the control points. In navigating between map and terrain, they *aim off*, *pace*, *check*, *contour*, find *at-* *tack points* and *catching features*. Each control point is marked with a control marker where the orienteer stops to stamp his or her control point card with a control clipper, to prove to officials at the finish that every control was reached. In *point*, *relay* or *line orienteering* control points must be reached in sequence. Courses are mapped by *course setter* or *planners*, and reviewed for accuracy by course *vetters*.

CONTROL POINT/CHECK POINT/ CONTROL

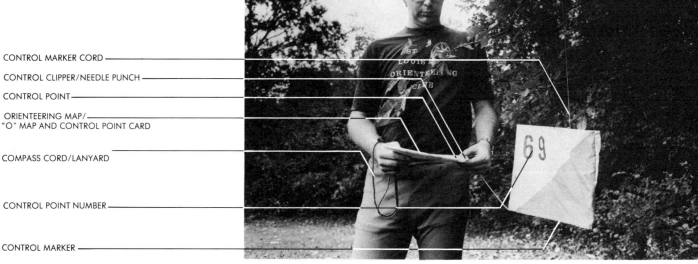

CONTROL MARKER CORD

CONTROL CLIPPER/NEEDLE PUNCH

CONTROL POINT

ORIENTEERING MAP/
"O" MAP AND CONTROL POINT CARD

COMPASS CORD/LANYARD

CONTROL POINT NUMBER

CONTROL MARKER

ORIENTEERING COMPASS/ PROTRACTOR-TYPE COMPASS

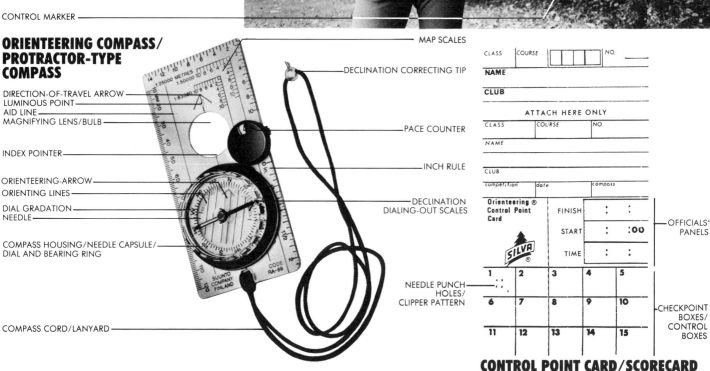

MAP SCALES

DECLINATION CORRECTING TIP

DIRECTION-OF-TRAVEL ARROW
LUMINOUS POINT
AID LINE
MAGNIFYING LENS/BULB

PACE COUNTER

INDEX POINTER

INCH RULE

ORIENTEERING-ARROW
ORIENTING LINES

DIAL GRADATION
NEEDLE

DECLINATION
DIALING-OUT SCALES

COMPASS HOUSING/NEEDLE CAPSULE/
DIAL AND BEARING RING

NEEDLE PUNCH
HOLES/
CLIPPER PATTERN

COMPASS CORD/LANYARD

OFFICIALS'
PANELS

CHECKPOINT
BOXES/
CONTROL
BOXES

CONTROL POINT CARD/SCORECARD

Platform tennis, or *'paddle,'* is an outdoor game, normally played in cold weather by *singles* players or by *doubles* teams. The rules are similar to tennis', except that only one service is allowed and the ball may be played off the side and back screens so long as it does not bounce on the deck a second time before being hit back, or *returned.* The clashing of partners' paddles in doubles does not make a return illegal, provided only one player strikes the ball.

Paddles are made of laminated wood or aluminum. The bright yellow ball is of firm sponge rubber.

Paddle tennis is played on a larger court with a punctured, or *'deadened,'* tennis ball.

PADDLE

HEAD (8¼" MAX.)
RIM/METAL RIM
HOLES (87 MAX.) ⅜" DIA.
FLUSH NUT & BOLT
HANDLE (6⅝")
KEEPER/ WRIST STRAP

BALL

WT. 2.3-2.5 OZ.
DIA. 2½"

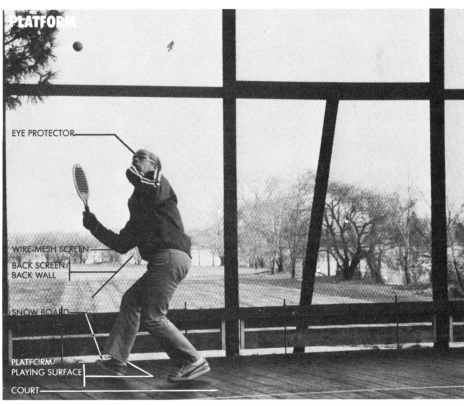

PLATFORM

EYE PROTECTOR
WIRE-MESH SCREEN
BACK SCREEN/ BACK WALL
SNOW BOARD
PLATFORM/ PLAYING SURFACE
COURT

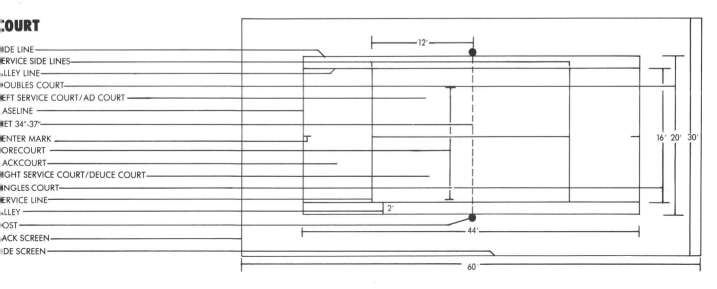

COURT

SIDE LINE
SERVICE SIDE LINES
ALLEY LINE
DOUBLES COURT
LEFT SERVICE COURT/AD COURT
BASELINE
NET 34"-37"
CENTER MARK
FORECOURT
BACKCOURT
RIGHT SERVICE COURT/DEUCE COURT
SINGLES COURT
SERVICE LINE
ALLEY
POST
BACK SCREEN
SIDE SCREEN

12'
2'
44'
60'
16' 20' 30'

Polo is played on horseback by two teams of four players each. Goals are scored by hitting the bamboo, ash, or plastic ball between the opponent's goal posts at any height. The mallet must be held in the right hand. The pony is controlled with the left hand.

A 7-minute period is a *chukker*. A game consists of eight such periods, known collectively as *chukkas*. Ties are broken in a *sudden-death chukker*, with the first score winning.

Players are numbered according to position. Forwards, numbered 1 and 2, play near the opposition's goal. Number 3 hits the ball upfield to the forwards. Number 4 protects the goal.

Two mounted *umpires* and a

ENGLISH SADDLE/POLO SADDLE

CANTLE/BACK ARCH
POMMEL/SADDLEBOW/HEAD
SKIRT
TREE/FRAME
KNEE ROLL/SWEAT FLAP
STIRRUP LEATHER BAR
FLAP
KEEPER
PANEL

POLO HELMET/CAP
CHIN STRAP
TEAM SHIRT
RIDING GLOVE
BREECHES
SADDLE
SADDLE BLANKET
BRAIDED TAIL
RIDING BOOT
KNEE GUARD
STIRRUP
TURF/FIELD

HEAD
SHAFT
MALLET/STICK 4½'
CLIPPED MANE
BRIDLE
BIT
BREAST PLATE
POLO SPURS
GIRTH & SURCINGLE
POLO & EXERCISE BANDAGE/FORELEG BANDAGE

PLAYER/POLOIST AND MOUNT/PONY/HORSE

POLO GROUND

GOAL MOUTH (8 YDS. WIDE)
GOAL POST (10' HIGH)
GOAL LINE/END LINE
30-YD. LINE
60-YD. LINE
300 YDS.
CENTER
FORWARDS
BACKS
PENALTY SPOT/40-YD. MARK
SIDE BOARDS/SIDE LINE/TOUCH LINE—11" HIGH
SAFETY ZONE
200 YDS.

referee on the sideline officiate. Polo players often ride a group of ponies, called a *string*, during a game.

Each player has a *handicap*, or rating, based on his record. In tournaments, these ratings are added to produce a *team handicap*. Extra points are given to weaker teams to equalize games.

During play, a player following the exact line of the ball, or pursuing it on a smaller angle than any other player, has the *right of way*.

Other players cannot interfere with him. But when players are riding after the ball in the same direction they may bump, or *ride off*, other players. Violations are penalized by the awarding of a goal or a free hit, depending on the foul.

STRETCH CALF
SLANTED FRONT POCKET
DOUBLE SEAT
RIDING BOOT

BREECHES

DIMPLE

3¼" DIA.

WT.: 4½ OZ.

BALL

UMPIRE
BACK'S STRIPE
POSITION NUMBER

Racquetball may be played by *singles* or two-person doubles teams. The object is to hit the ball off the front wall so that an opponent cannot return it before it bounces twice. A rally also ends when a *hinder* is called. *Avoidable hinders* are intentional interference and are penalized by loss of point or serve. *Unavoidable hinders* and *court hinders*, in which the ball is unintentionally obstructed, result in replays.

A ball may hit any wall or walls or the ceiling before hitting the front wall, but may not hit the floor.

A game is 21 points. Points may only be scored by the serving team. A serving team losing a rally loses the serve. A match is two out of three games.

RACQUET

COURT

9"

GUARD
FRAME
STRINGS

HEAD
13.5"

GRIP/HANDLE

BUTT

WRIST THONG/STRAP

CEILING (IN PLAY)
SIDE WALL
RECEIVING LINE/
5-FOOT LINE
BACK WALL

FRONT WALL

SERVICE LINE
SERVICE ZONE (5' WIDE)
DOUBLES SERVICE BOX
SHORT SERVICE LINE

20'
HIGH

12' HIGH
(MINIMUM)

40' LONG

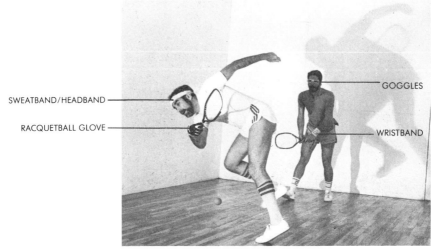

SWEATBAND/HEADBAND
RACQUETBALL GLOVE

GOGGLES

WRISTBAND

2¼" DIA.

RACQUETBALL
WT: 1.4OZ.

A rodeo is an exhibition of *cowboy skills* in which contestants, or *eventers*, demonstrate their ability to control livestock, or *stock*.

Judges score, or *mark*, an eventer's overall control of his animal, his *ride*, which requires both *spurring* and *reining*. The response of the stock to the rider, *stock performance*, is scored separately and is based on *kicks* and *jumps*.

Principal events are saddle bronc riding, bareback bronc riding, bull riding, calf roping and steer wrestling. Other competitions include barrel racing, *wild-horse racing* and *wild-cow milking*. Eventers are usually permitted two or more attempts in each event, the winner compiling the highest score or lowest time.

BAREBACK BRONC RIDING

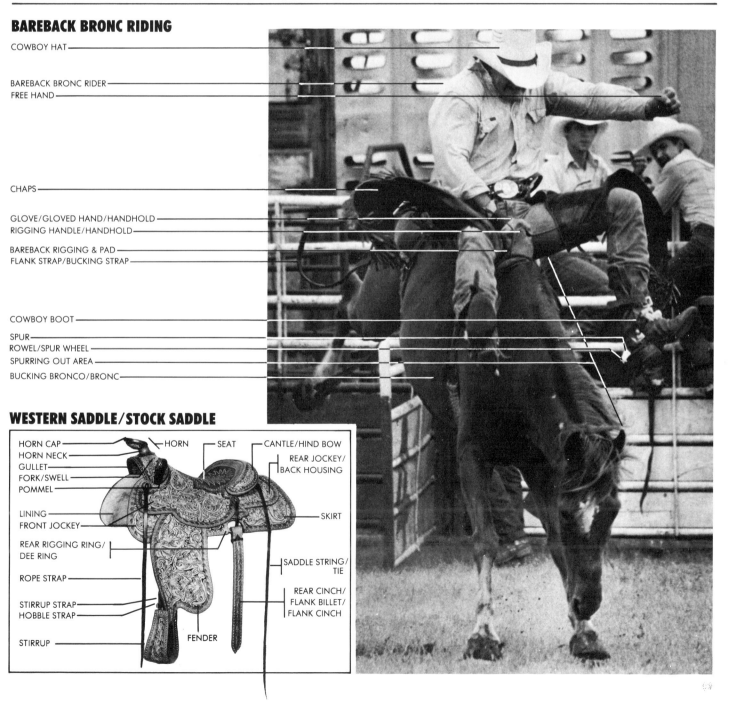

COWBOY HAT

BAREBACK BRONC RIDER
FREE HAND

CHAPS

GLOVE/GLOVED HAND/HANDHOLD
RIGGING HANDLE/HANDHOLD

BAREBACK RIGGING & PAD
FLANK STRAP/BUCKING STRAP

COWBOY BOOT

SPUR
ROWEL/SPUR WHEEL
SPURRING OUT AREA
BUCKING BRONCO/BRONC

WESTERN SADDLE/STOCK SADDLE

HORN CAP
HORN NECK
GULLET
FORK/SWELL
POMMEL

HORN

SEAT

CANTLE/HIND BOW

REAR JOCKEY/
BACK HOUSING

LINING
FRONT JOCKEY

REAR RIGGING RING/
DEE RING

ROPE STRAP

STIRRUP STRAP
HOBBLE STRAP

STIRRUP

FENDER

SKIRT

SADDLE STRING/
TIE

REAR CINCH/
FLANK BILLET/
FLANK CINCH

Bronc riders are allowed a *single handhold* on the reins. A rider who *'pulls leather,'* or touches the saddle with his free hand during his eight-second ride, is disqualified.

Bull riders also ride for eight seconds using a single handhold.

After a rider is thrown, *rodeo clowns* attract the bull from him.

A calf roper ropes the stock from horseback, dismounts, throws the calf to the ground and ties three of its legs together for a five-second count, timing to begin after he

remounts.

Steer ropers slide off their *mounts* onto a steer and wrestle it to the ground.

Barrel racers lose five seconds for each barrel they knock over.

SADDLE BRONC RIDING

HALTER & HORSE'S CHAMPION TITLE
BUCKING REIN/BRONC REIN/BUCK REIN
SADDLE BRONC RIDER

BULL RIDING

BULL
BULL RIDER
FLANK STRAP/BUCKING STRAP
CHUTE/BUCKING CHUTE

COWGIRLS BARREL RACING

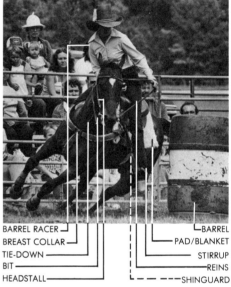

BARREL RACER
BREAST COLLAR
TIE-DOWN
BIT
HEADSTALL
BARREL
PAD/BLANKET
STIRRUP
REINS
SHINGUARD

BARREL RACING COURSES

BARRELS

LEFT-TURNING HORSE COURSE

RIGHT-TURNING HORSE COURSE

STEER WRESTLING/'BULLDOGGING'

HAZER
RODEO PLANT/RODEO ARENA
STEER WRESTLER
STEER

TEAM ROPING

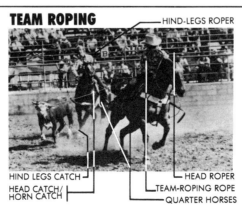

HIND-LEGS ROPER

HIND LEGS CATCH
HEAD CATCH/HORN CATCH
HEAD ROPER
TEAM-ROPING ROPE
QUARTER HORSES

CALF ROPING

PIGGIN' STRING
CALF-ROPING ROPE/LARIAT
QUARTER HORSE
CALF

Artistic roller skating consists of three separate competitive entities: figure, free and dance.

Figure skating, similar in nature to the *compulsory figures* in ice skating, requires mastery of standard edges and turns in executing prescribed patterns.

In dancing, all competing couples perform a prescribed set of steps to the same music. All movements must be performed in unison. They are judged by the accuracy of their steps and by their ability to interpret the rhythm of the music.

Movements and choice of music in free skating are left up to the skater. Performances are judged by the speed and height of *jumps*, the control and velocity of *spins*, and the individuality of *footwork*.

FREE SKATING
CAMEL SPIN

DANCE SKATING
LIFT/ONE-ARM REVERSE KENNEDY

LIFT BEGINS WITH MAN BENDING BOTH KNEES, KEEPING BACK STRAIGHT. THE WOMAN LOCKS BOTH ARMS.

KEEPING HEAD UP AND BACK ARCHED, THE MAN LIFTS THE WOMAN UP OVER THE CENTER OF HIS HEAD.

THE WOMAN KEEPS HER BODY RIGID AND HER HEAD DIRECTLY OVER THE MAN'S AS HER HAND IS RELEASED.

IN THE FINAL LIFT POSITION, THE MAN AND THE WOMAN EACH EXTEND THEIR FREE ARM DURING FOUR ROTATIONS.

Unlike ice hockey, roller hockey is a non-contact game whose rules are similar to soccer's. If the ball goes out of play, for example, it is put back into play with a *free hit*.

International speed skating involves *sprints* and *distance races* on either a 200-meter banked track or on an *'open'* or *'closed circuit'* road *race course*. In the U.S., indoor racing takes place on a 100-meter flat, oval track, with distances determined by age and sex. Outdoor road races, for skaters age fourteen and up, are conducted on a 300-meter flat, oval track made of asphalt.

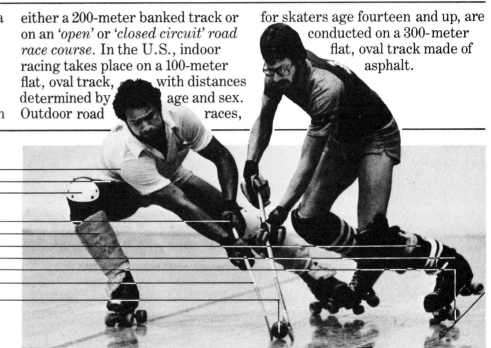

ROLLER HOCKEY

SHIRT
SHORTS
KNEE PAD

PADDED GLOVE
SHIN GUARD
SOCK
HOCKEY BOOT
ROLLER SKATE
STICK (3–3¾′ LONG)
BALL : CIRC. 9 IN.
WT. 5½ OZ.

RINK

GOAL
GOALIE
CREASE
GOALKEEPER'S PENALTY LINE
PENALTY AREA
DEFENSEMEN

BASE SPOT CIRCLE
BASE SPOT
PENALTY SPOT
RINK BARRIER (8″ HIGH)
FORWARDS

CENTER CIRCLE
CENTER LINE

18 FT.

40½ FT.

SKATE

TONGUE
TOE CUP/
TOE BOX

BOOT
HEEL

TOE STOP
PIVOT

WHEEL
AXLE
AXLE NUT
BALL BEARINGS

SOLE PLATE

ACTION NUT/LOCK NUT
CUSHIONS
KING PIN/ACTION BOLT/TRUCK BOLT

TRUCK

SPEED SKATING TRACK

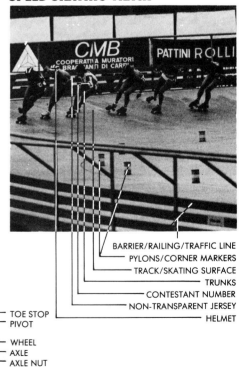

BARRIER/RAILING/TRAFFIC LINE
PYLONS/CORNER MARKERS
TRACK/SKATING SURFACE
TRUNKS
CONTESTANT NUMBER
NON-TRANSPARENT JERSEY
HELMET

International competition is comprised of sculling, in which one, two or four *scullers* propel *racing shells* called sculls by simultaneously pulling on two oars mounted on opposite sides of the boat, and rowing, in which two, four or eight *oarsmen* each use single oars.

A *regatta*, or *sprint*, is conducted in *heats* over a six-lane course laid out on a straight stretch of still water. Boats not placing high enough to qualify for the final heat are allowed to compete again in a second-chance heat called a *repechage*.

In *head of the river races*, competitors starting at intervals are timed over a course too narrow to accommodate all *crews*.

SCULLING HEAT

CATCH

DRIVE/PULL THROUGH

FINISH & RECOVERY

SCULLING TECHNIQUE

SCULL DETAIL

Rowing races are contested in cox-less pairs and four-man boats, and coxed pairs, fours and eight-man boats. Many regattas have separate competition for heavyweight crews and *lightweights* (consisting of crews averaging no more than 150 pounds per person).

An eight-man shell may be up to 60 feet long. The sliding seat and the outrigger, which extends the *pivot point* of the oar outboard of the shell, allows the oarsman to use back and legs as well as arms in pulling the oar through a long, powerful arc, or *sweep*.

An oarsman is said to '*catch a crab*' if the feathered tip of his oar digs into the water during the recovery phase of a stroke.

The coxswain steers the shell.

SHELL

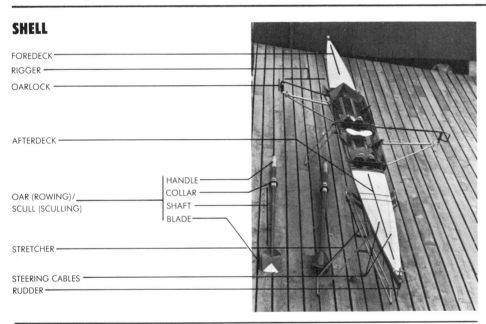

FOREDECK
RIGGER
OARLOCK
AFTERDECK
OAR (ROWING)/
SCULL (SCULLING)
HANDLE
COLLAR
SHAFT
BLADE
STRETCHER
STEERING CABLES
RUDDER

COXSWAIN/COX
#7 OAR
STROKE/#8 OAR
#5 OAR
#6 OAR
#3 OAR
#4 OAR
BOW OAR/#1
#2 OAR
SHELL

EIGHT-MAN CREW

SWEEP-ROWING TECHNIQUE

CATCH

DRIVE/PULL THROUGH

RELEASE AND FEATHER

RECOVERY

Amateur rugby, *rugby union*, is played by 15-man teams. Professional rugby, *rugby league*, is played by 13-man teams. The object of the game, generally played in two 40-minute *halves* with no time outs or substitutions, is to carry the ball into the opponent's 'in goal area' and touch it to the ground (called a *try*, worth 4 points), or *dropkick* or *placekick* the ball over the *crossbar* and between the *goal posts* (called a *goal*, or *dropped goal*, worth 3 points).

The ball may only be kicked or run forward, but may be passed laterally. When the ball carrier is *tackled*, he must release the ball. For common infractions, a scrum is formed and the ball put back into play.

SCRUM

JERSEY

13½–15½ OZ.
11"–11¼" LONG — BALL
24"–25½" CIR.

SHORTS

STOCKING/SOCK

BOOT

PITCH/FIELD

DEAD BALL LINE

DEAD BALL ZONE

GOAL LINE/
TRY LINE

5 YDS.

TOUCH LINE

10 YARDS LINE

10 YDS.
MAX.

HALF-WAY LINE

25 YARDS LINE

18'6"
10' GOAL

25 YDS.
MAX.

75 YDS. MAX.

SCRUMMAGE FORMATION

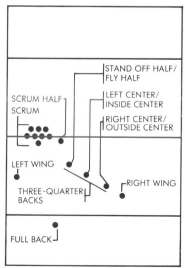

STAND OFF HALF/
FLY HALF

SCRUM HALF/
SCRUM

LEFT CENTER/
INSIDE CENTER

RIGHT CENTER/
OUTSIDE CENTER

LEFT WING

RIGHT WING

THREE-QUARTER
BACKS

FULL BACK

SCRUM POSITIONS

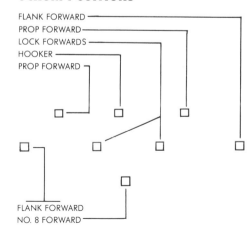

FLANK FORWARD
PROP FORWARD
LOCK FORWARDS
HOOKER
PROP FORWARD

FLANK FORWARD
NO. 8 FORWARD

Rifle events are divided into *small-bore* and *bigbore* rifles (the *bore* being measured in *calibers*, bore diameter in 100ths or 1000ths of an inch), and *air rifle*, powered by compressed air or CO_2 cartridge. Shooting positions include prone, bench rest, sitting, standing, and kneeling, in which a cylindrical *kneeling pad*, or *roll* may be used. In *running game target* shooting, 60 shots are fired at a simulated boar, moving on rails at slow speed for 30 shots and at high speed for the remaining 30. This is the only event in which *telescopic sights* are allowed.

The competitor with the highest score wins.

SHOOTING POSITIONS

BENCH REST

PRONE

STANDING/OFF-HAND

KNEELING

SITTING

RUNNING GAME TARGET SHOOTING/ RUNNING BOAR

Pistol shooting is comprised of *free pistol, rapid-fire pistol* and *small-bore sport pistol*. In each event the pistol may be held unsupported with only one hand and the competitor must stand.

In free pistol, competitors are allowed 2½ hours to take six *series* of 10 shots each at small targets with scoring rings valued from one to 10. A shot that hits one of the scoring ring boundaries scores the higher value.

In rapid-fire, or *silhouette* shoot-ing, 60 shots are fired in groups of five, each at five different targets that pop up simultaneously when the competitor calls *"Ready."* Smallbore sport pistol is a combination of free-and rapid-fire, with 30 shots fired in each.

NATIONAL MATCH TARGET PISTOL

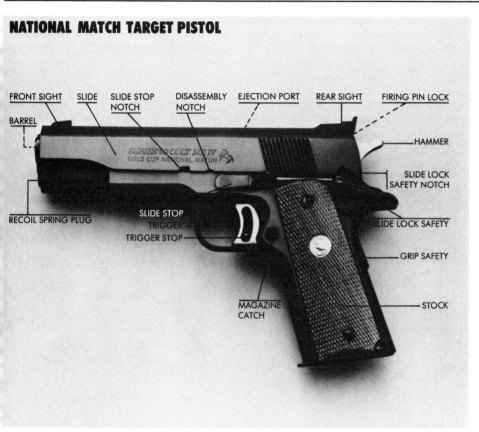

FRONT SIGHT · SLIDE · SLIDE STOP NOTCH · DISASSEMBLY NOTCH · EJECTION PORT · REAR SIGHT · FIRING PIN LOCK

BARREL

HAMMER

SLIDE LOCK SAFETY NOTCH

RECOIL SPRING PLUG

SLIDE STOP
TRIGGER
TRIGGER STOP

SLIDE LOCK SAFETY

GRIP SAFETY

MAGAZINE CATCH

STOCK

CARTRIDGE/BULLET

CASE HEAD · RIM · BULLET/SLUG/HEAD · CRIMP · JACKET · NOSE

PRIMER · CASE

TARGET

SCORING BOX

'BLACK'

BULLSEYE · POINT VALUE

PISTOL RANGE

BULLET BARRICADE/RICOCHET FENCING/'BERM'

MAIN BACKSTOP · DEFLECTOR · EARTHWORKS

160' (FREE PISTOL)
82' (RAPID FIRE PISTOL & SMALLBORE SPORT PISTOL)

TARGET NUMBER · TARGET · SWIVEL MOUNT · TARGET FRAMES

FIRING STATION

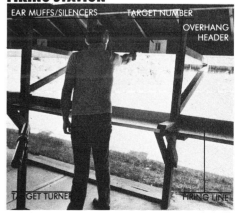

EAR MUFFS/SILENCERS · TARGET NUMBER

OVERHANG HEADER

TARGET TURNER · FIRING LINE

In trapshooting, also called *trench shooting*, a competitor shoots at five targets from each of five stations.

Targets are launched on command, whenever the gunner calls *'pull.'* The birds are thrown in varying directions by three traps located opposite each shooting station in the trap pit, or trench.

Competitors load two *cartridges* into their shotguns and may use both if the target is missed on the first shot. Three *misfires* are allowed each competitor in a round. If the target is launched before the shooter's call or not immediately thereafter, it is called *'no bird'* and a new target is allowed.

SHOTGUN — COMB/FORECOMB, SMALL OF STOCK/PISTOL GRIP, RECEIVER, BREECHBLOCK, EXTRACTOR, VENTILATED RIB, BORE, STOCK/BUTTSTOCK, BUTT PLATE, HEEL, MAGAZINE CAP, BARREL, SAFETY, TRIGGER, TRIGGER GUARD, LOADING GATE, FOREARM/FORE-END/SLIDE HANDLE, MAGAZINE TUBE, CHECKERING, STOCK GRIP CAP, TOE

SCORER & PULLER, POWER HOOK-UP, 49'3", TRAP HOUSE, TRAP RELEASE/PULLING MECHANISM, FIRING STATION

TRAPSHOOTING RANGE

TARGET TRAJECTORY, 125 MPH, 49'3", HANDICAP DISTANCE MARKERS

Shotguns are used in trap and skeet shooting events to down saucer-shaped targets called *clay pigeons*, *clays*, or *birds*. To score a hit, the *gunner* must break the target, which is flung into the air by a *trap* to simulate the take-off flight of a *game bird*.

In skeet shooting, targets thrown from the high house follow a horizontal trajectory, those from the low house are thrown on a rising path. In a *round*, which consists of 25 shots, a competitor fires from eight positions at 16 targets thrown alternately from the two houses, then fires from four of the positions at eight targets thrown by both houses simultaneously. The 25th shot is taken at any time in the round.

MARKSMAN

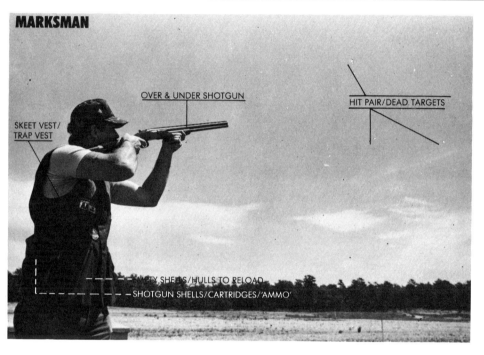

SKEET VEST/ TRAP VEST
OVER & UNDER SHOTGUN
HIT PAIR/DEAD TARGETS
EMPTY SHELLS/HULLS TO RELOAD
SHOTGUN SHELLS/CARTRIDGES/'AMMO'

TARGETS/CLAYS/BIRDS/PIGEONS

RIM
DOME
OUTLINE
4⅓" DIA.
WT: 3.7 OZ.

SKEET RANGE

TRAP HOUSE/ HIGH HOUSE
TRAP HOUSE/LOW HOUSE
18'
90 MPH
63'
FIRING STATIONS
JUDGES' STAND

SKEET & TRAP MACHINE/TRAP
HORIZONTAL TARGET TRAJECTORY
RISING TARGET TRAJECTORY
TRAP HOUSE/ LOW HOUSE
SHOOTER IN 'SHOOTING POSITION'
TRAP HOUSE/HIGH HOUSE
TRAP
BASE CHORD (120.9')
NEXT SHOOTER UP
SHELL BAG/ AMMO POUCH
RELEASE CABLE
RANGE
FIRING STATION
PULLER

Shuffleboard players attempt to push wood or composition disks so that they stop within one of five *scoring areas* in the triangle. (Disks touching lines do not count.) Ten points are deducted for disks stopping in the 10-off area. Each player pushes four red or black disks, and may knock opponents' disks from one area to another, or out of play. Scores are tallied after each player has pushed his or her four disks. The area from which play begins is the *head* of the court, and disks are pushed toward the *foot*. In doubles, a member of each team plays from the baseline of either triangle.

Games may be 21, 50, 75 or 100 points, as desired. A *match* is the best two out of three games.

COURT

DISK

NEUTRAL ZONE

DEAD LINES

SCORING DIAGRAM/SCORING TRIANGLE

10-OFF SQUARE/MINUS SQUARE

SEPARATION TRIANGLE

BASE LINE

BACKSTOP

GUTTER

PLAYER

CUE

COURT NUMBER

6" DIAMETER
11½-15OZ.

RUNNER/GLIDE

FORK

SHAFT

CUE

There is no standardized course or field on which competitive skateboarding is staged. Events are adapted to whatever space is available. *Vertical*, *full-pipe* or *half-pipe*, or *bowl riding* events take place in an area with banked or vertical sides, such as an empty swimming pool. Contestants are judged on the radicalness of their tricks, continuity and style. Judging in *flat freestyle* events is similar. In the *slalom*, skateboarders race against the clock over a designated course, weaving between cones. Speed on a skateboard is controlled by movement of the body forward and backwards.

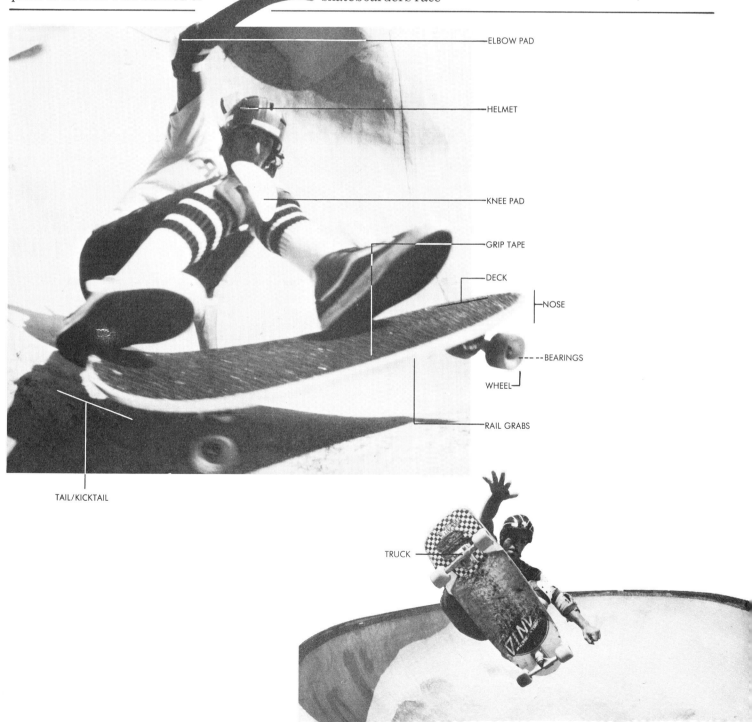

ELBOW PAD

HELMET

KNEE PAD

GRIP TAPE

DECK

NOSE

BEARINGS

WHEEL

RAIL GRABS

TAIL/KICKTAIL

TRUCK

Alpine skiing consists of *downhill*, *slalom* and *giant slalom*. The fastest event, in which skiers follow the *fall line* as closely as possible in the crouched, *egg position*, is the downhill. In slalom, competition is decided by the fastest aggregate

time down two different, twisting *courses* containing *open* and *closed gates*. Giant slalom combines the speed of downhill with the turning skill of slalom. The event is similar to slalom except that the course is longer, with gates further apart.

The ideal *line* through gates is not necessarily the shortest distance between them. Racers approach gates from a *high position*, enabling them to make rounded turns that reduce the need for braking.

THE SKIER

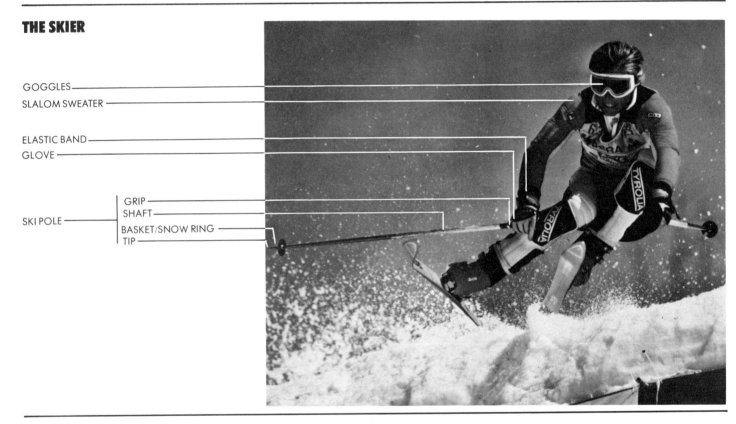

GOGGLES

SLALOM SWEATER

ELASTIC BAND

GLOVE

SKI POLE —
GRIP
SHAFT
BASKET/SNOW RING
TIP

STARTING GATE

STARTING HUT

WISHBONE STARTING GATE

WAND

COURSE/PISTE

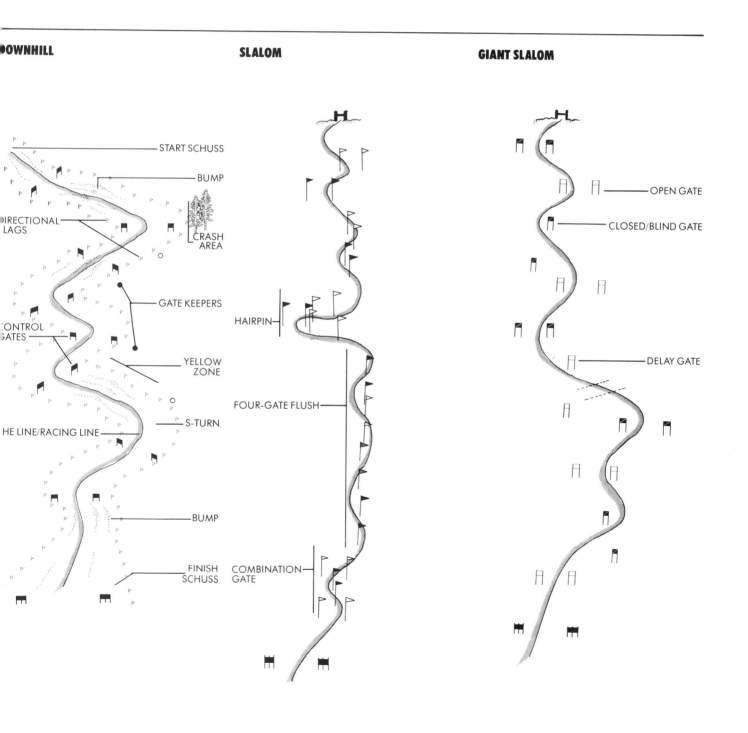

DOWNHILL

SLALOM

GIANT SLALOM

START SCHUSS

BUMP

DIRECTIONAL FLAGS

CRASH AREA

GATE KEEPERS

CONTROL GATES

YELLOW ZONE

THE LINE/RACING LINE

S-TURN

BUMP

FINISH SCHUSS

HAIRPIN

FOUR-GATE FLUSH

COMBINATION GATE

OPEN GATE

CLOSED/BLIND GATE

DELAY GATE

EQUIPMENT

HELMET/CRASH HELMET

- SHELL
- CHIN PIECE
- EDGE TRIM
- CHIN STRAP RIVET
- AIR VENTS

- CUFF PADDING
- TONGUE
- CLOSURE

BOOT

- FLEX ADJUSTER
- CUFF
- HINGE
- SOLE
- BUCKLES
- TONGUE SHELL
- SHELL
- CUFF

BINDING

- HEEL HEIGHT ADJUSTMENT SCREW
- HEEL CUP
- TOE HEIGHT ADJUSTMENT SCREW
- TOE CUP
- TOE-PIECE RELEASE SETTING INDICATOR
- RELEASE ADJUSTMENT SCREW
- POLE EXIT SOCKET
- MANUAL RELEASE
- RELEASE ADJUSTMENT SCREW
- HEEL RELEASE SETTING INDICATOR
- BRAKE BASE
- SKI BRAKE
- HEEL PIECE
- ANTI-FRICTION PAD
- TOE PIECE

SKI

- TAIL
- WAIST
- SHOULDER
- SHOVEL
- SIDEWALL
- TIP

FINISH AREA

- GATE
- SNOW FENCE
- HAY BALE
- FINISH BANNER
- LIGHT SOURCE
- FINISH LINE
- TIMING/CALCULATIONS HUT
- PHOTOCELL
- RESULT BOARD
- RUNOUT AREA/OUTRUN AREA
- PRESS AREA
- FLAGGED ROPE

Nordic skiing encompasses cross country racing, ski jumping and *Nordic Combined*, which includes both events.

Ski jumpers are permitted two jumps in competition. They are scored on *distance* and *style*, or *form*. Five *style judges* may award as many as 20 points, but high and low scores are eliminated. These points are added to points for distance, which are awarded based on the number of meters jumped, for a total.

Jumping skis are longer, wider and heavier than alpine skis. They have no edges and may have built-in *air scoops*. Ski jumpers wear streamlined suits with no protective padding.

ONE-PIECE JUMP SUIT
BIB/ENTRY NUMBER
GLOVE

HELMET
GOGGLES

JUMPING SKI
TRACKING/GROOVES

JUMPING BOOT

CABLE BINDING/
'BEAR TRAP' BINDING

VORLAGE POSITION

JUMPING HILL

STARTING GATE
IN-RUN
(94-112 YDS. LONG)
TOWER WITH
WARMING ROOMS
(66 YDS. HIGH)
TRACK
CHIEF OF TAKE-OFF
TAKE-OFF POINT/LIP
KNOLL
METER MARKERS
LANDING HILL
(77-99 YDS. LONG)
NORM POINT
TABLE POINT
CRITICAL POINT
JUDGE'S TOWER
(STOP AND GO LIGHTS,
WIND DIRECTION,
SPEED CALCULATIONS,
SCOREBOARD)
TRANSITION CURVE
OUT-RUN
(88-110 YDS.
LONG)

JUMPER

IN-RUN POSITION

TAKE-OFF POSITION

AIR FLIGHT POSITION/
AIR FOIL POSITION

TELEMARK LANDING POSITION

OUT-RUN
POSITION

Cross country racers start 30 seconds apart and race against the clock on a *trail* composed of uphill, flat and downhill sections. A second track alongside the main trail is used for passing, but skiers must give way upon request. There are individual and relay races for men and women, with distances ranging from about 3 miles to 9½ miles.

Biathlon contestants pause several times during their cross country ski run to shoot at targets. They shoot from both a prone and a standing position. Penalty minutes are added to a contestant's final time for each miss. In some events, laps must be skied on a penalty course for each miss. The contestant with the fastest adjusted time wins.

CROSS COUNTRY SKIER

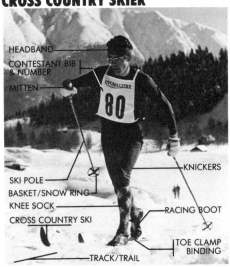

HEADBAND
CONTESTANT BIB & NUMBER
MITTEN
80
KNICKERS
SKI POLE
BASKET/SNOW RING
KNEE SOCK
RACING BOOT
CROSS COUNTRY SKI
TOE CLAMP BINDING
TRACK/TRAIL

BIATHLON TARGETS

1'6"   1'2"   5"   10
STANDING   PRONE

TOE CLAMP BINDING

TOE CLAMP
SKI
finngrip
LEVER
TOE PINS

RACING BOOT

LIP/EXTENDED TOE
TOE PIN HOLES

STANDING POSITION

CHEEK PIECE
EYESHADE
.22 RIFLE
REAR SIGHT
FRONT SIGHT
PROTECTIVE CAP
HARNESS
SLING
MAGAZINE POUCH BELT
FIRING POINT NUMBER
CROSS COUNTRY SKI

PRONE POSITION

R
TARGET BOARD/ PRONE TARGETS
164'

Soccer is played by two 11-man teams on a field of grass or hard clay. The object is to drive the ball past the opposing goalkeeper into the goal for a score, worth one point. The team with the most *goals* at the end of two 45-minute periods of play, or halves, wins. In the event of a tie, or *draw*, regulation play is extended by a 15-minute, first goal wins, *sudden death* overtime, or by a series of *penalty kicks*, called a *shootout*.

The only *footballer* allowed to use his hands while the ball is in play is the goalkeeper. All others must use their feet, thighs, chests or heads to control, pass and to shoot the ball. Only two substitutions are allowed in a game, or *match*, and no time-outs.

At the start of play, each team must stay in its own half of the field, with defending players remaining at least 10 yards away from the ball until it has been kicked forward at least 27 inches by the opposition. When one team drives the ball out of bounds across a sideline, the other team puts it back in play with a *throw in*. If the attacking team drives it over the other's goal line, the defending team puts it back in play with a *goal kick*, from the goal area. If it was last touched by the defending team, a *corner kick* is awarded to the attackers.

Since no rules govern player positions, their makeup depends on game tactics and strategy.

FIELD/PITCH

BASIC FORMATIONS

4-2-4

4-3-3

Players are not permitted to hold, push or trip an opponent, but they may bump him with a shoulder charge and use their feet in an effort to *tackle*, or take the ball away from an opponent. For rules violations (such as touching the ball with a hand) or for fouls, the offending team is penalized by the awarding of a *direct* or *indirect free kick* to the opposition. In an indirect kick the attacker may not score a goal without a second player touching it first. The player taking the direct free kick may score directly. If a defending player commits a foul in his own penalty area, the opposition is awarded a penalty kick, taken from the penalty spot with only the goalkeeper allowed to defend.

PLAYING THE BALL

HEADING · TRAPPING · JUGGLING · DRIBBLING

FOULS

DANGEROUS PLAY

TRIPPING

CHARGING

HOLDING

OFFICIALS' SIGNALS

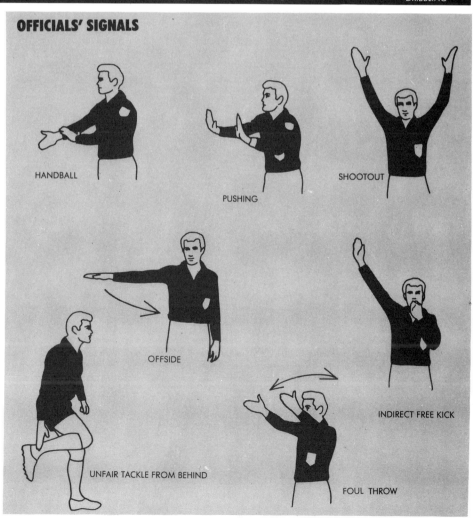

HANDBALL · PUSHING · SHOOTOUT · OFFSIDE · INDIRECT FREE KICK · UNFAIR TACKLE FROM BEHIND · FOUL THROW

Softball is popular as both a recreational and highly organized sport for men and women. The rules and terminology are similar to those of baseball, but pitchers must throw underhand, the dimensions of the field and the size of the ball differ, and games are only seven innings long.

Two distinct versions of softball are played. In *slow pitch*, the pitcher throws the ball in a three- to 10-foot arc at moderate speed. A 10th player, called a *short fielder*, or *rover*, usually plays between the infielders and outfielders. Bunting and base stealing are prohibited.

In *fast pitch*, the pitcher may throw as hard and as fast as he or she is able, so long as the ball is released from below hip level.

METAL BAT
WT: 38 OZ. (MAX.)
2¼" DIA. (MAX.)

COVER STITCHES

DYNA CORE

SOFTBALL
12"–12⅛" CIR.
WT: 6¼-7 OZ.

BARREL

34" (MAX.)

RUBBER GRIP

KNOB

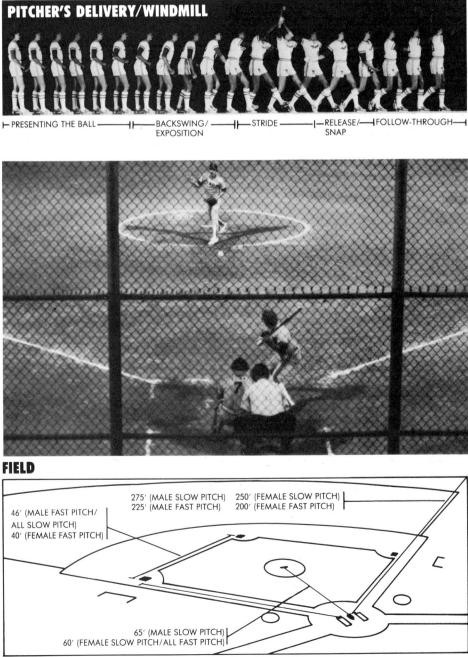

PITCHER'S DELIVERY/WINDMILL

├─ PRESENTING THE BALL ─┤├─ BACKSWING/ ─┤├─ STRIDE ─┤├─ RELEASE/ ─┤├─FOLLOW-THROUGH─┤
                          EXPOSITION   SNAP

FIELD

275' (MALE SLOW PITCH)   250' (FEMALE SLOW PITCH)
225' (MALE FAST PITCH)   200' (FEMALE FAST PITCH)

46' (MALE FAST PITCH/
ALL SLOW PITCH)
40' (FEMALE FAST PITCH)

65' (MALE SLOW PITCH)
60' (FEMALE SLOW PITCH/ALL FAST PITCH)

SPEED SKATING

159

Olympic or metric style skating consists of two skaters competing at the same time on a 400-meter *track*, *rink*, or *oval*. A *staggered start* ensures that both skaters race the same distance. After the first *lap*, skaters cross over each time they make a full circle. Since skaters race against the clock, winning does not necessarily mean beating the other person.

In non-Olympic "pack" style meets, skaters race in crowded *heats*. *Short track speed skating* consists of *individual*, *team relay* and two-skater *pursuit races*.

RINK

SNOW RIDGES/LANE MARKERS

START 3000, 5000   START 1000   STARTER   START 1500

CROSSING CONTROLLER/FLAGMAN

CROSSOVER STRAIGHT/
CROSSING ZONE/
BACKSTRETCH

JUDGE   JUDGE

CURVE

CHIEF TIMEKEEPER
LAP SCORER
FINISH STRAIGHT

TIMEKEEPER
FINISH LINE JUDGE

INNER LANE
OUTER LANE

PRESTART LINE   START 500   FINISH 1000   FINISH 500, 1500, 3000, 5000, 10000

SKATER

HOOD

ZIPPER
THUMB HOLE

STIRRUP

SKATE

REINFORCING

BOOT

HEEL PLATE
HEEL CUP
SPOT WELD
BLADE/RUNNER

TONGUE
EYELET

SPORT SHOELACE

SOLE PLATE
TOE STANCHION
SOLE CUP
TUBE

In squash, a singles or doubles game played in a four-walled court, the object is to hit the ball to the front wall in such a way that an opponent may not return it to the wall before it bounces twice.

Under international rules, games are played to 9 points and only the serving side may score. If the server fails to keep the ball in play, the serve passes to the opponent.

In the American version, played to 15 points, both server and receiver may score points.

Squash tennis, similar to squash racquets, is played with a larger, highly pressurized ball and a larger, heavier racquet, making it a faster game.

COURT

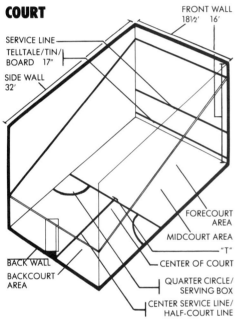

FRONT WALL 18½' 16'
SERVICE LINE
TELLTALE/TIN/ BOARD 17"
SIDE WALL 32'
FORECOURT AREA
MIDCOURT AREA
"T"
CENTER OF COURT
BACK WALL
BACKCOURT AREA
QUARTER CIRCLE/ SERVING BOX
CENTER SERVICE LINE/ HALF-COURT LINE

RACKET

HEAD THROAT SHAFT GRIP/HANDLE
27" MAX.
7¼" 8½" STRINGS

BALL

1.6" DIA.
WT. .68–.77 OZ.

FRONT WALL
CORNER
TELLTALE

Competitive surfing rules vary from beach to beach. Generally, however, surfers are required to ride a certain number of waves in specified time periods, called *heats*. The surfer who executes the most radical ma- neuvers in the most critical sections of the biggest waves for the longest distance is deemed the winner.

The area where surfers straddle their boards waiting for waves to begin curling is called '*the lineup*.'

Riding a board while completely enclosed by the pipeline is '*tubing*.' The object is to ride the tube before it '*closes out*,' or collapses. A '*regular foot*' stands with his left foot forward. '*Goofy foots*' take a reverse stance.

ANATOMY OF A WAVE

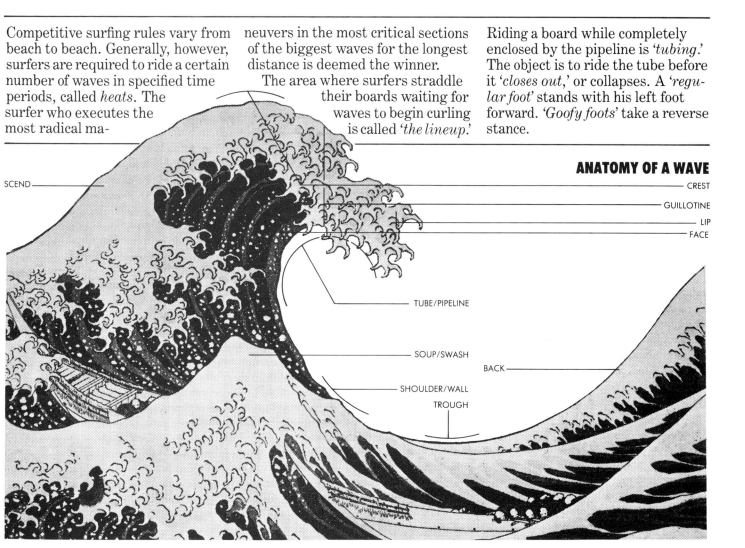

SCEND
CREST
GUILLOTINE
LIP
FACE
TUBE/PIPELINE
SOUP/SWASH
BACK
SHOULDER/WALL
TROUGH

SURFER

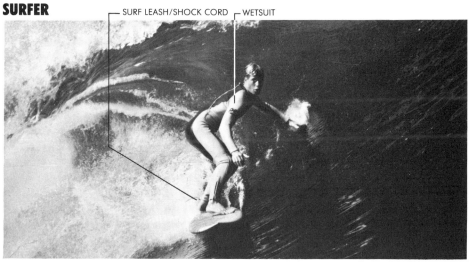

SURF LEASH/SHOCK CORD — WETSUIT

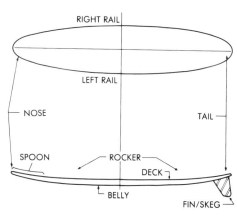

RIGHT RAIL
LEFT RAIL
NOSE
TAIL
SPOON
ROCKER
DECK
BELLY
FIN/SKEG

SURFBOARD/BOARD

Synchronized competition, or *synchro*, consists of two parts: *compulsory figures*, done without music and judged on skill and technique, and *routines*, performed to music and judged on presentation and showmanship. Seven judges award 0-10 points for each performance by solo, duet and eight-swimmer teams.

In compulsories, which count for about 50% of the total score, each contestant performs six figures chosen from a possible 46 by officials. In routines, a series of basic movements choreographed into a graceful balletic presentation, swimmers may spend half their time upside down in the water. Underwater speakers help keep them in synch with the music.

BASIC POSITIONS

BACK LAYOUT   BENT KNEE   BALLET LEG   FLAMINGO   BALLET LEG DOUBLE POSITION   CRANE   FRONT PIKE   SPLIT

BACK PIKE   TUCK   FISHTAIL   VERTICAL   KNIGHT/CASTLE   BENT KNEE   SIDE   FRONT

Eight-lane Olympic pools, considered 'fast pools,' are designed to minimize two types of waves that check swimmers' speed. *Surface tension waves* are controlled by lane marker *discs* that spin and absorb kinetic energy and by overflow gutters that keep water from 'sloshing' back into competitors' lanes. *Gravity waves*, generated by the force of swimmers going through the water, bounce off the bottom and are reflected upwards. The depth of the pool allows the swimmer to get past the point where the gravity wave resurfaces.

The recall rope is for *false starts.* The individual responsible for the third false start is disqualified, or *DQ'd*.

POOL

EVENTS & ENTRY BOARD
AUTOMATIC SCOREBOARD
STARTER
OVERFLOW GUTTER
DIVING TANK
REFEREE
RECALL ROPE
WASH LANE
BACKSTROKE TURNING LINE/FLAG LINE

POOL DECK
ELECTRONIC TIMING EQUIPMENT

TURN

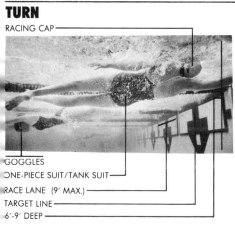

RACING CAP
GOGGLES
ONE-PIECE SUIT/TANK SUIT
RACE LANE (9' MAX.)
TARGET LINE
6'-9' DEEP

START

END WALL
BACKSTROKE START HANDGRIP
STARTING BLOCK
FASTEST QUALIFYING SWIMMERS
STARTER

LANE MARKER DISCS
LANE LINE
LANE MARKER

Individuals compete by sex in the following events: *freestyle*, *butterfly*, *backstroke*, *breaststroke* and *individual medley*, in which competitors swim equal distances in each of four strokes. Team events include *medley relay* and *freestyle* *medley*.

In freestyle races, swimmers may choose any style or stroke. The crawl is preferred since it is fastest. At turns and at the finish the swimmer may touch the wall with any part of the body.

In butterfly, the second fastest stroke, arm and leg movements must be simultaneous, and shoulders must be parallel to the surface of the water at all times. At turns and finishes the swimmer must touch the wall with both hands

CRAWL/FRONT CRAWL

BUTTERFLY

BACK CRAWL

BREASTSTROKE

at the same time and at the same level.

The third fastest event is the backstroke which is started in the water, with hands on the starting platform's grips and feet placed under the water against the end wall. Although no particular style is required for the backstroke, except that it be performed on the back, most swimmers prefer the back crawl for its speed.

In breaststroke the body must be kept parallel to the surface of the water, and arms and legs must be pushed and pulled simultaneously and symmetrically. Like butterfly, touches at turns and at the finish must be made at the same time and at the same level.

CRAWL/FRONT CRAWL

BACK CRAWL

BUTTERFLY

BREASTSTROKE

Table tennis is played by individuals or two-player teams. The object is to hit a hollow celluoid or plastic ball over a net so that it cannot be returned after one bounce by the receiver.

A player or team serves five times, then the opposition serves five times, and so on. A game is 21 points, unless tied 20-20, then the first player or team to gain a 2-point advantage wins.

Players also lose points for *volleying*, or striking the ball before it hits the table on their side, for touching the table with their free hand during a *rally* (the period the ball is in play), or for touching the ball before it goes out of bounds.

PLAYING SURFACE/TABLE TOP
COURTS
NET
SUPPORT POST
TENSION ADJUSTMENT KNOB
SUSPENSION CORD
TAPE
MESH
6" HIGH
WING NUT
CLAMP
SIDE LINE
RAIL
LEG BRACE/LEG HINGE
5'
20' MIN.
PLAYING AREA
40' MIN.
9'
LEG
2'6"
CENTER LINE/DOUBLES LINE
END LINE/BASE LINE

PADDLE/RACKET/BAT

BLADE/HEAD
BALL
THROAT/NECK
1½" DIA.
WT: .1 OZ.
FACE/PIMPLED RUBBER/STRIKING SURFACE
SANDWICH
THE WOOD

SERVICE/PUTTING BALL IN PLAY

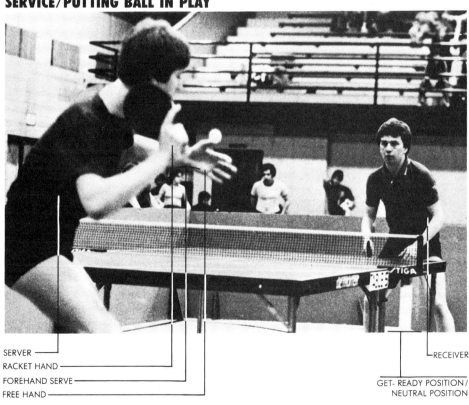

SERVER
RACKET HAND
FOREHAND SERVE
FREE HAND
RECEIVER
GET-READY POSITION/NEUTRAL POSITION

GRIPS

ORTHODOX/SHAKEHANDS

PENHOLDER/ORIENTAL

After 15 minutes of play, the *Expedite System* is used. Under these rules each player or team serves once, then the opposition serves, and so on. If the receiver returns serve and 12 succeeding shots successfully, he or she wins the point.

A *let*, a rally in which no point is won, occurs when the serve touches the net but is otherwise playable, or if the serve is delivered when the receiver is not ready, or if an official interrupts play, or if an accident not caused by either player occurs and play is stopped.

The racket may be of any size, weight or shape.

DEFENDER/CHOPPER/RETRIEVER

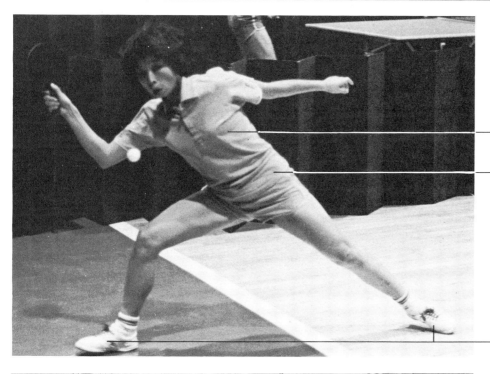

PLAYING SHIRT

PLAYING SHORTS

TABLE TENNIS SHOES/PLAYING SHOES

RETURN

FOREHAND FOLLOW-THROUGH

SMASH/KILL SHOT/PUTAWAY

DEFENSIVE POSITION

TABLE NUMBER

COURT

Tennis, also called *lawn tennis*, is played by two individuals (*singles*) or pairs (*doubles*) on a grass, clay, asphalt or composition court divided by a low net. Players using rackets hit a ball over the net with the object of making a shot that lands within the boundaries of an opponent's court but that cannot be returned before it bounces twice.

Play is started by one player, standing behind the baseline, serving diagonally across the court into his opponent's service court. A serve that hits the net tape but falls into the appropriate court is a *let*, and is taken again. A serve into the net or out of the service court is a *fault*, and a second serve is taken. Although players serve alternate games, both serving and receiving

CENTER COURT/CENTRE COURT

SCOREBOARD
BALL BOY
LET JUDGE/NET JUDGE
UMPIRE/CHAIR UMPIRE

LINE JUDGE/LINE UMPIRE
FAULT JUDGE/FAULT UMPIRE
FAULT JUDGE/FAULT UMPIRE
LINE JUDGES/LINE UMPIRES

sides can score points.

Zero, or no points is called *love*. The first point is 15, although it is also called 5. The second is 30, the third is 40, the fourth is *game*. However, when both sides score 40, it is called *deuce*. With the score tied at deuce a game may go on indefinitely, since a player or team must take a two-point lead to win.

The first player to win six games wins a *set*, unless each has won five. A two-game margin is then required to win the set. A *match* is best of three sets, except in men's championships which is best of five sets.

COURT

RIGHT SERVICE COURT/DEUCE COURT
DOUBLES SIDELINE
ALLEY 4½'
SINGLES SIDELINE
FORECOURT

CENTER LINE
LEFT SERVICE COURT/AD COURT
CENTER MARK
SERVICE LINE
BACKCOURT
BASELINE

36'
27'
39'
TAPE
NET POST
NET 36" HIGH
CENTER STRAP/ NET ANCHOR
21'
18'

RACKET
WT. 13-15 OZ.

9"
CROWN
TIP
CROSS STRINGS
FACE
MAIN STRINGS
HEAD
BINDING/ TRIM TAPE
SHOULDER
THROAT
SHAFT
27"
HANDLE/GRIP
HEEL

SPALDING
IMPACT JUNIOR

BALL

2-2½ OZ.
2½"–2⅝" DIA.

NAP
SEAM

SWEET SPOT

A server is generally considered to have an advantage in a game because he controls the beginning of each point and because the ball in a serve is not hit on the fly or on the run. If a player serves the ball so well that his opponent cannot even touch it, called an *ace*, he wins the point automatically. If, on the other hand, he fails to serve well and loses the game, he is said to have had his serve *broken*.

In serving, *ball placement* (deep in an opponent's service court corners) is most important. A serve can, in addition, be made more difficult to *return* if it is *angled* or *spun*, or hit flat with a great deal of speed, called a *cannonball*.

READY POSITION   BACKSWING   TOSS   CONTACT   FOLLOW-THROUGH

TYPES OF SERVE

X

TWIST

SLICE

FLAT

All *shots* may be offensive or defensive in nature, depending on *court position*, skill and tactics.

Shots in which the ball is hit after bouncing are called *ground strokes* and consist of forehand and backhand. A *half-volley* is made immediately after the ball strikes the playing surface. A volley is hit near the net in mid-air with little or no *backswing*. An *overhead*, or *overhead smash*, is a stroke that resembles a serve but which may be hit anywhere within the court.

A *chop* is hit with a short, downward stroke which imparts backspin to reduce the ball's bounce and makes it *die*. A *chip* is an angled chop, aimed at an opponent's feet.

FOREHAND

VOLLEY

STROKES

CROSS-COURT SHOT   DOWN-THE-LINE SHOT

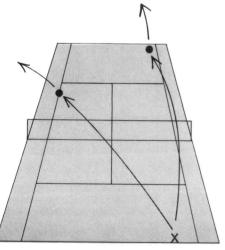

BASELINE POSITION

NO-MAN'S LAND

NET POSITION

KNOCKOUT ZONE/ VOLLEY & OVERHEAD ZONE

ATTACK ZONE/HALF-VOLLEY & MID-COURT OVERHEAD ZONE

UNBALANCING ZONE/ PRE-ATTACK ZONE

PASSING SHOTS   **COURT ZONES**

Tactics in tennis include mixing speed and spin in various shots, which makes the ball more difficult to return and puts an opponent on the defensive. In a flat shot, or *drive*, for example, the ball takes a level bounce. A ball hit with topspin travels faster and bounces higher after making contact with the court, whereas a backspin shot is intended to reduce the ball's momentum when it bounces.

There are two kinds of lob. A *defensive lob*, hit very high, gives a player time to get back into position. An *offensive lob* is hit over an opponent's head, out of reach.

A *putaway*, *kill*, or *winner*, is any hard hit shot that cannot be returned.

THE BOUNCE

LOBS

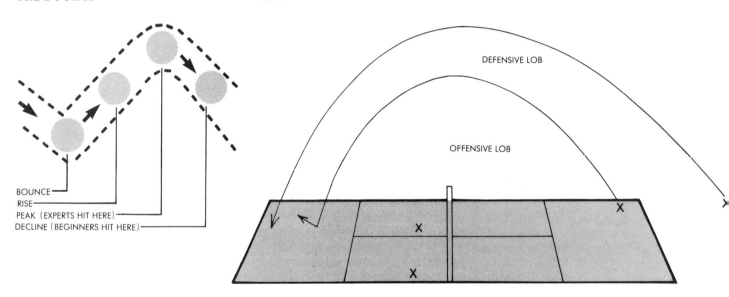

BOUNCE
RISE
PEAK (EXPERTS HIT HERE)
DECLINE (BEGINNERS HIT HERE)

DEFENSIVE LOB

OFFENSIVE LOB

BALL SPIN

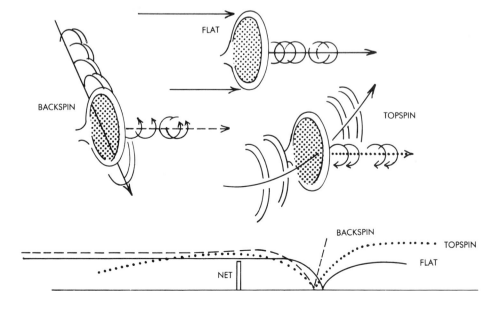

FLAT

BACKSPIN

TOPSPIN

BACKSPIN
TOPSPIN
FLAT

NET

Track and field is comprised of running, jumping and throwing events for men and women. *Track meets* are held both indoors and outdoors. In most events competitors wear lightweight shorts, T-shirts or *singlets*, and shoes designed especially for specific contests.

Both men and women compete in sprints and distance races, hurdle races and relays (at different distances), the shot put, discus, high jump and long jump.

Generally, only men compete in the steeplechase, race walking, hammer throw, pole vault and triple jump, although on occasion these events are held for women.

Track events take place on an oval track. Field events take place inside the track.

SCOREBOARD   TURN   FINISH LINE FOR ALL RACES
STRAIGHTAWAY
LANES

QUARTER-MILE (CIR.) TRACK   STAGGERED STARTING AREA   FIELD EVENTS AREA   STEEPLECHASE WATER JUMP   33½'   RELAY EXCHANGE ZONE   CHUTE/SPRINTS STARTING LINE   TUNNEL (MARATHON EXIT & ENTRY)

Sprints are run indoors and outdoors on oval tracks at distances of 100-, 200- and 400-meters. In races that make use of turns on the track, a *staggered start* is used to insure that all runners cover the same distance.

The first *sprinter* to break the vertical plane of the finish line with his or her torso wins.

Sprinters must stay in their lanes throughout the race. They cannot leave the track or obstruct other runners. Violators are disqualified.

Two *false starts*, or leaving the blocks before the starter fires his gun, also disqualify a competitor.

If there are numerous *entries*, qualifying races, or *heats*, are held to limit the final *field*.

STARTING BLOCKS

PIN/ANCHOR

ADJUSTMENT SCREW/BLOCK LOCK

RAILS

FACE

BLOCK/PEDAL

END PIECE

FINISH LINE

TAPE/FINISH TAPE

4'

2"

INSIDE LANE/POLE POSITION

STARTING TECHNIQUE

STARTING COMMAND: 'ON YOUR MARK'

'SET'

GO POSITION

ACCELERATION

UPRIGHT POSITION

In relay races, each of the four runners on a team covers the same distance consecutively. As each runner finishes, he or she passes a baton to the next runner.

Men and women's Olympic relays are run at 4x100- and 4x400-meters, but other meets include relays at most middle and long distances. *Medley races*, in which each runner covers a different distance, are also run on occasion.

The baton must be exchanged in the 22-yard-long passing zone. If dropped in the zone, either runner may retrieve it. If dropped outside the zone, the racer who dropped it must pick it up.

The first anchor man to cross the plane of the finish line wins.

BLIND PASS

BATON

4¾" CIR.   11"–12"

WT: 1¾ OZ. (MIN.)

PASSING ZONE

SECOND MAN

THIRD MAN   SCRATCH MARK   PASS MADE TO SECOND MAN

PASS MADE TO THIRD MAN

SCRATCH MARK (WHEN INCOMING RUNNERS REACH THIS POINT, NEXT MAN BEGINS RUNNING)

START: LEAD-OFF MAN RUNS FIRST LEG

SCRATCH MARK

ANCHOR MAN

PASS MADE TO ANCHOR MAN (TO FINISH)

PASSING TECHNIQUES/HANDOFFS

RUNNER'S DIRECTION

UPWARD THRUST/UPSWEEP

DOWNWARD THRUST/DOWN PASS

The number of hurdles runners must pass over, the distance between them and their height varies according to race distance. *Indoor hurdlers* must clear four hurdles in the 50-yard dash, five in the 60 and six in the 70. In all outdoor races, including the decathlon and heptathlon events, runners must clear 10 hurdles.

Hurdlers must stay in their own lanes throughout the race. There is no penalty for accidentally knocking over a hurdle, but racers are disqualified for trailing a foot or leg alongside a hurdle, jumping a hurdle in the wrong lane or deliberately knocking over a hurdle with a hand or foot.

The first racer clearing all hurdles to cross the finish line wins.

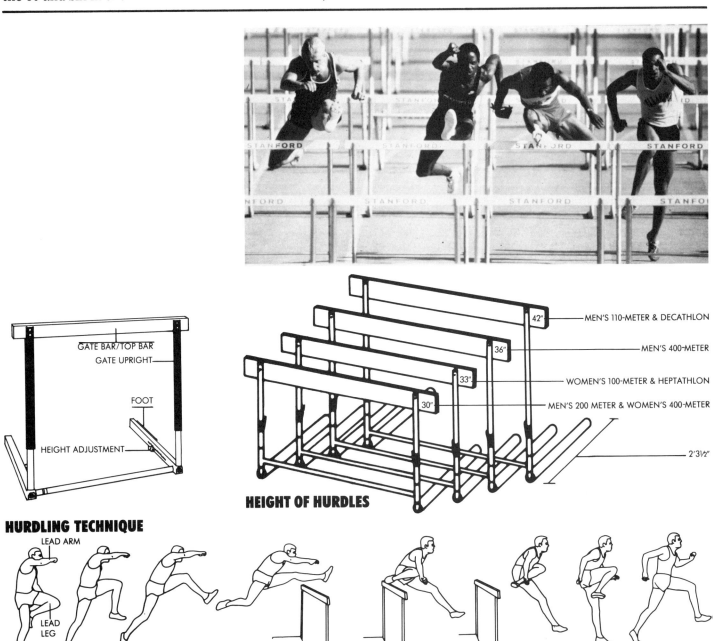

GATE BAR/TOP BAR
GATE UPRIGHT
FOOT
HEIGHT ADJUSTMENT

42″ — MEN'S 110-METER & DECATHLON
36″ — MEN'S 400-METER
33″ — WOMEN'S 100-METER & HEPTATHLON
30″ — MEN'S 200 METER & WOMEN'S 400-METER
2′3½″

HEIGHT OF HURDLES

HURDLING TECHNIQUE

LEAD ARM
LEAD LEG
TRAILING LEG

The steeplechase is a 3,000-meter (240 yds. less than two miles) race, consisting of seven laps around a track, during which runners go over 28 dry hurdles and seven water jumps.

Runners may clear hurdles by jumping over them, using one hand to vault over, or, as most runners do, landing on top of the bar with one foot and leaping off to land in the shallowest water.

Steeplers are disqualified for going around a jump, failing to go through or over the water, or trailing a foot or leg alongside any hurdle.

Racers wear shoes with perforations to allow drainage.

The first runner to cross the finish line with his torso wins.

DRY HURDLE

CROSSBAR/BAR 5"

3'

UPRIGHT

12'

WT: 176–220 LB.

BASE

WATER JUMP

TRAILING LEG

12'

12"

5"

3'

Men's and women's distance races cover 800 meters (half-mile), 1500 meters (metric mile) and the marathon distance. Women also run a 3000-meter race, while men compete at 5000 and 10,000 meters.

The 800-meter run begins from a staggered start and racers must stay in their lanes for the first two turns. All other races begin from a single starting line and runners may run wherever they choose. Many prefer the inside, or *pole lane*. In all running and walking races, the first competitor to break the vertical plane of the finish line with his or her torso wins.

The marathon covers 26 miles, 385 yards. Competitors may use any running or walking step to cover that distance. The taking of

RUNNING SHOE

HEEL PATCH/
ACHILLES'
TENDON PAD
PADDING
BINDING
TONGUE
EYELETS
EYE STAY
LACES

TOE BOX
VAMP
TRIM
UPPERS
OUTSOLE

THE 'PACK' COMING AROUND A TURN

refreshments and sponging off are permitted at official stations. Special 'ultra-marathons', covering distances as long as 100 miles, are also run but are not generally part of any track and field meet.

Race walks are held at various distances, ranging from one mile to 75,000 meters, with men's olympic races held at 20 and 50 kilometers.

Race walkers must have part of one foot in contact with the ground at all times, i.e., the rear foot cannot leave the ground until the front foot has touched. The leg must also be momentarily straightened while the foot is on the ground. If three or more judges believe a walker is running, he is disqualified.

MARATHON START

RACE WALKING TECHNIQUE

Javelin throwers are permitted six attempts, with the longest single throw winning. Ties are broken by comparing second best efforts.

The javelin must be thrown overhand. It cannot be hurled or slung. The thrower may go outside the runway lines during the approach, but must be between them and behind the arc when releasing the *jav*.

Crossing the arc before the javelin lands is a foul, nullifying the throw.

The point of the javelin must hit the ground first or the throw does not count, although the point does not have to stick in the ground. The throw is measured from the mark made by the point to the intersection of the sector lines.

Four judges officiate.

JAVELIN

(MEN) 8'10¼"
WT: 1 LB. 12 OZ.

(WOMEN) · 7'6½"
WT: 1 LB. 5 OZ.

SHAFT

CORD
GRIP

HEEL SPIKES   HEEL WEDGE

JAVELIN SHOES

THROWING SECTOR

40 YDS. — 311'6" — SECTOR FLAG

RUNWAY/APPROACH
13'1½"

29°

MEASUREMENT POINT
(TO MARK MADE BY JAVELIN)

ARC/FOUL LINE/SCRATCH LINE/TOE BOARD   SECTOR LINE

THROWING TECHNIQUE

BOW POSITION   RELEASE   FOLLOW THROUGH
& RECOVERY

APPROACH/CARRY POSITION   CROSSOVER STEP   RELEASE   WHIPCRACK

Shot putters may use any body motion to put, or push, rather than throw the shot, so long as they start from a stationary position and the one hand used for putting never goes lower than it does at the starting position.

Competitors are permitted six attempts, with the longest single effort winning. Ties are broken by comparing second best puts. Distance is measured from the inner edge of the ring to the nearest mark made by the shot, and rounded off to the lowest quarter-inch.

Shot putters may touch the inside face of the raised toeboard, but if they touch its top, or the area beyond the ring, the attempt is nullified.

SHOT PUT SHOES

BUMPER

SHOTS

(MEN)
16 LB.
5" DIA.

(WOMEN)
8 LB. 13 OZ.
4¼" DIA.

PHOTO BY WALTER IOOSS JR. FOR 'SHOOTING FOR THE GOLD' © 1984 FUJI PHOTO FILM USA

SHOT PUTTING SECTOR

SECTOR FLAG

SECTOR LINE

SHOT PUT RING/CIRCLE

45°

DIVIDING LINE

FOUL LINE

7'

4"

STOPBOARD/TOEBOARD

75'5"

PUTTING TECHNIQUE

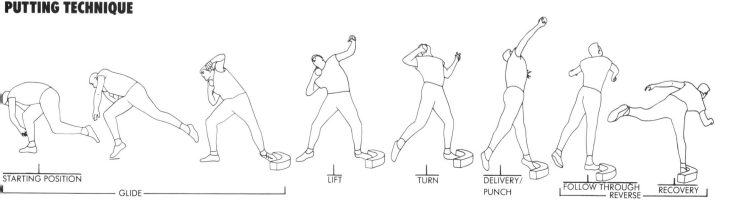

STARTING POSITION

GLIDE

LIFT

TURN

DELIVERY/
PUNCH

FOLLOW THROUGH
REVERSE

RECOVERY

Both discus and hammer throwers compete from inside a steel wire or fiber netting cage designed to catch errant throws.

Throwers in both events are given six attempts (although some competitors may be eliminated after three *qualifying throws*), with the longest single throw winning. Ties are broken by comparing second-best throws.

In both events throws are nullified if the competitor steps on or beyond the outer ring, leaves the ring before the discus or hammer has landed, fails to leave the ring from behind the dividing line, or if the throw lands outside the throwing sector.

Throws are measured from the inner edge of the ring to the nearest

DISCUS

RIM

BODY

WEIGHT

(MEN)
WT: 4 LBS. 6.5 OZ.
8.6" DIA. 1¾" WIDTH

(WOMEN)
WT: 2 LBS. 3.2 OZ.
7" DIA. 1½" WIDTH

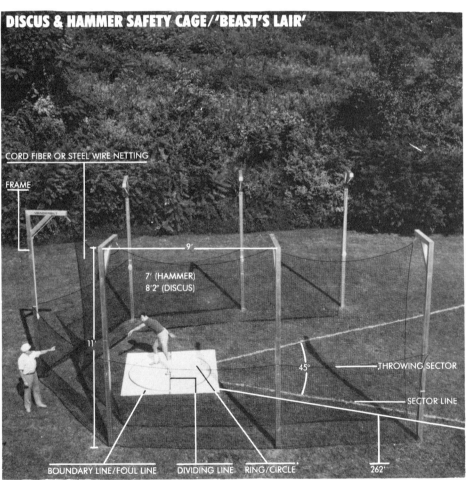

DISCUS & HAMMER SAFETY CAGE/"BEAST'S LAIR"

CORD FIBER OR STEEL WIRE NETTING

FRAME

9'

7' (HAMMER)
8'2" (DISCUS)

11'

45°

THROWING SECTOR

SECTOR LINE

BOUNDARY LINE/FOUL LINE   DIVIDING LINE   RING/CIRCLE   262'

THROWING TECHNIQUE

PIVOT/TURN/SPIN/ROTATION

DELIVERY/RELEASE   FOLLOW THROUGH
REVERSE

mark made by the discus or the head of the hammer, and rounded off to the lowest inch.

Throwers must begin from a stationary position. The discus may be held and thrown by any method. The head of the hammer may touch the ground during preliminary swings.

Only men compete in the hammer throw. The entire hammer apparatus, including head, wire and handle is thrown. If the hammer breaks during a throw, that trial does not count against the competitor.

Five judges officiate, two watching for infringements within the ring, and three making sure the throw lands within the sector lines.

HAMMER

1/8"

GRIP
HANDLE

WIRE

'10¼"–3'11¾"
WT: 16 LBS.

SWIVEL

–4¾"

HEAD/BALL
(BALL WT: 15 LBS.)

HAMMER GLOVE

THROWING TECHNIQUE

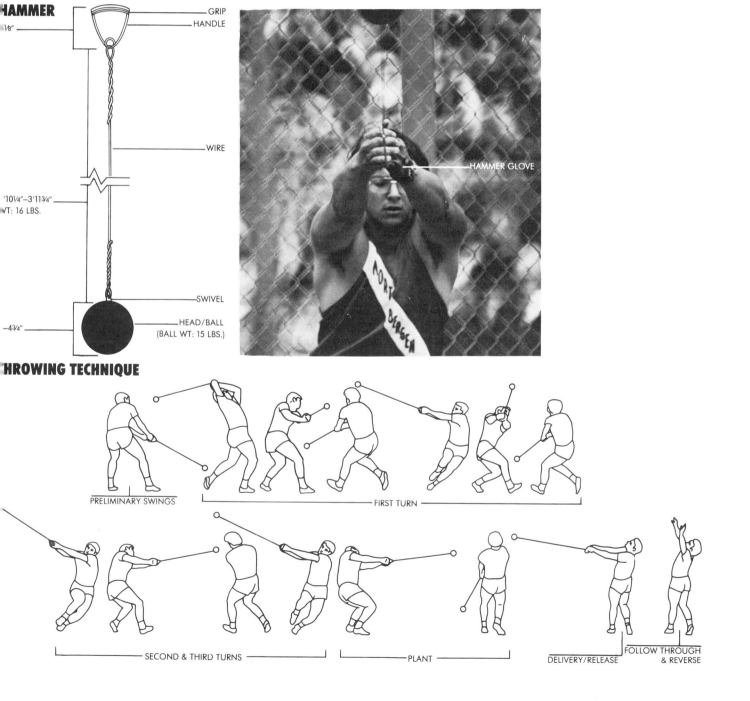

PRELIMINARY SWINGS

FIRST TURN

SECOND & THIRD TURNS

PLANT

DELIVERY/RELEASE

FOLLOW THROUGH
& REVERSE

Long jump and triple jump competitors may make as long a run-up as desired. If they touch the ground beyond the takeoff line it is a *foul*, and the jump is nullified.

Jumpers make six attempts, with the longest single jump winning.

Ties are broken by comparison of the second longest jumps.

Jumps are measured from the nearest mark, or *break*, made in the sand or sawdust by any part of the body to the takeoff line, and rounded off to the nearest quarter inch.

In the hop portion of the triple jump, jumpers must land on the same foot with which they hit the take-off board, and to complete the step must land on the other foot. The jump is nullified if they touch ground with the wrong foot.

JUMPING AREA

RUNWAY 130' (APPROX.)

4'

TRIPLE JUMP TAKE-OFF

4'

LONG JUMP TAKEOFF

TAKE-OFF BOARD
TAKE-OFF LINE
FOUL LINE/
PLASTICINE INDICATOR

3'3"

33' (APPROX.)

LANDING PIT
(SAND OR
SAWDUST)

9'

LONG JUMP/BROAD JUMP TECHNIQUE

FREE LEG

HITCH KICK

BOUNCE-OUT

RUN-UP   TAKE-OFF   FLIGHT   LANDING

HOP, STEP AND JUMP TECHNIQUE

'SLEEPING
FOOT'

HANG
POSITION

LANDING POSITION

TAKE-OFF   TAKE-OFF   TAKE-OFF

HOP   STEP   JUMP

High jumpers may begin competing at any height they choose above the minimum set by the judges, and then elect to pass at subsequent heights. A jumper is eliminated after three successive failures.

A jump is a failure if the jumper knocks the bar off its supports, steps into the landing area before clearing the bar, or takes off from both feet.

Final standings are determined by the greatest height cleared by a jumper. If jumpers tie, the jumper with the fewest misses wins.

Bar height is measured from take-off point to the lowest point on the upper side of the bar.

The main styles used are the flop, in which the jumper goes over the bar on his back, and the straddle.

HIGH JUMP (FLOP) SHOE

PLASTIC HEEL CUP
ADDED COLLAR
HEEL SPIKES

FLOP

Photo by Walter Iooss for Shooting For the Gold © 1984 Fuji Photo Film U.S.A.

JUMPING AREA

LANDING AREA/LANDING PIT
UPRIGHT/STANDARD
8'4"
13'2"
CROSSBAR SUPPORT
RUN-UP/RUNWAY/FAN
16'4"
CROSSBAR/BAR

STRADDLE/ROLL

TRAIL LEG
LEAD LEG

RUN-UP/APPROACH ⎿ TAKE-OFF ⏋ ⎿ CLEARANCE ⏋ ⎿LANDING⏌

FIELD
POLE VAULT

186

Pole vaulters use flexible poles to loft themselves over a crossbar. Vaulters may choose to jump or pass at any height, but if they elect to jump and fail on three attempts at a given height they are eliminated. The bar is raised after each vaulter has jumped or passed at a specific height. The winner is the vaulter who has cleared the greatest height. In case of ties, the vaulter with the fewest misses wins.

Poles may be of any length and diameter, and made of any material, although fiber glass 'sky poles' are favored.

If a vaulter knocks the crossbar off its supports, changes hands in mid-air, or touches the pit with the pole, the vault is a failure.

VAULTING TECHNIQUE

CARRY — SHIFT — PLANT

TAKE-OFF — SWING AND ROCK BACK — PULL — PUSH OFF AND CLEARANCE

FLIGHT

DECATHLON AND HEPTATHLON/COMBINED EVENTS

The 10-event decathlon, or *all around*, for men, and seven-event heptathlon for women, are tests of various track and field skills. Contested over two days, they require *decathletes* and *heptathletes* to demonstrate proficiency in running, jumping, endurance and strength sports.

Athletes compete against a predetermined standard in each event rather than against each other. Points are added or subtracted by comparing the athlete's effort to the set standard. In running, for example, points are deducted for each fraction of a second the competitor is slower than the set standard. Events do not carry equal value in the total score. Highest total points wins.

MEN'S EVENTS   **WOMEN'S EVENTS**

100-METER DASH

LONG JUMP

SHOT PUT

HIGH JUMP

400-METER DASH

DISCUS

110-METER HURDLES

POLE VAULT

JAVELIN

110-METER HURDLES

HIGH JUMP

200-METER DASH

SHOT PUT

LONG JUMP

JAVELIN

METRIC MILE RUN

Numerous officials are necessary to run a track meet. Races are begun by a *starter* firing a gun. The starter also rings a bell at the beginning of the last, or *bell*, lap. A *recall starter* watches for premature movement. The *timer* clocks races,

and *finish line judges* determine the order in which runners place.

In throwing events, two *judges* by the ring watch for violations, while two or more near the sector lines help measure distance and insure the throw lands within bounds.

Two *judges* control the high jump and three work the pole vault. Four oversee the long jump and a fifth is added for the triple jump.

The *clerk of the course* schedules races. The *scorer* tabulates results.

MEASUREMENT IN INCHES
CASE
TAPE
WIND-UP ARM/REEL & LOCKING DEVICE
HOOK
TAPE MEASURE

COMPUTERIZED PERFORMANCE INDICATOR
JAVELIN — EVENT
COMPETITOR ATTEMPT PLACE
354 2 1
PERFORMANCE
99.72
DISTANCE (METRIC & ARABIC)
STANDING AT TIME

STARTER'S PISTOL/GUN

WIND INDICATOR
WIND
+15
WIND TO COMPETITOR'S BACK
WIND SPEED (MPH)

FIELD EVENT TIMER
GREEN (TIMED PERIOD HAS BEGUN)
YELLOW (30 SECONDS REMAINING)
RED (TIME EXPIRED/ TRIAL NULLIFIED)

TIMER
START/STOP, SPLIT/ RESET BUTTONS
CUM TIME/ CUMULATIVE TIME DISPLAY FONT
LAP TIME
SPEED KEY
KEYPAD
RECALL KEY

LONG JUMP & TRIPLE JUMP MEASURING DEVICE

SCOPE
DIGITAL READOUT
SLIDE
RAIL

STOPWATCH
BOW
CROWN/START & STOP BUTTON
RESET BUTTON
MINUTE HAND
SECOND HAND
SECOND BITS
BEZEL
SPORT CRAFT
1/10 TH
⅒ SECOND BITS

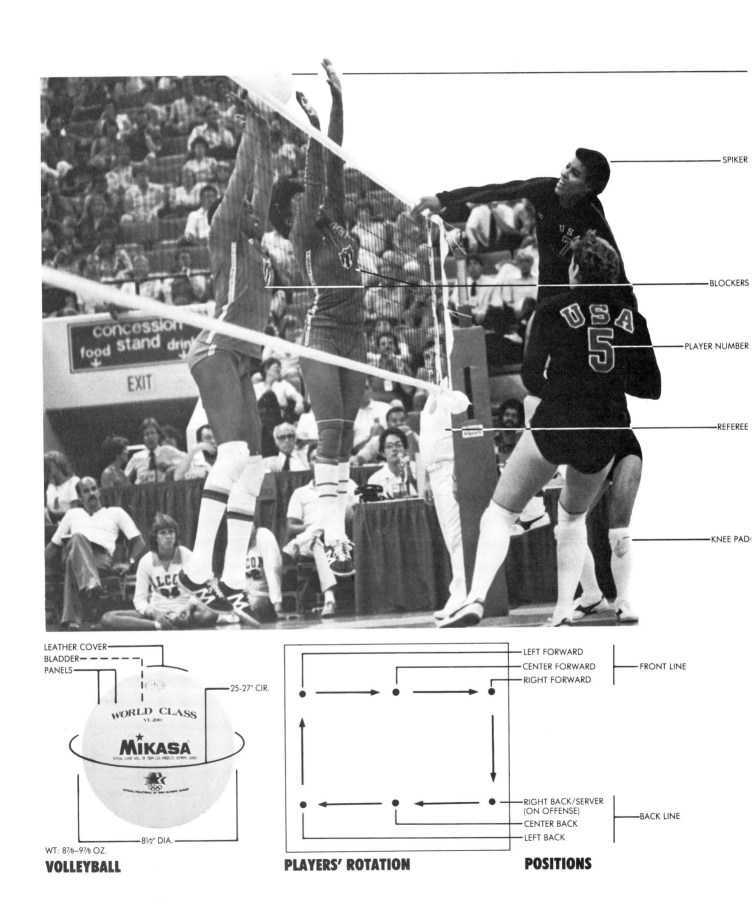

SPIKER

BLOCKERS

PLAYER NUMBER

REFEREE

KNEE PAD

LEATHER COVER
BLADDER
PANELS

25-27" CIR.

WORLD CLASS
VL 200

MIKASA

8½" DIA.

WT: 8⅞–9⅞ OZ.

VOLLEYBALL

LEFT FORWARD
CENTER FORWARD — FRONT LINE
RIGHT FORWARD

RIGHT BACK/SERVER
(ON OFFENSE)
CENTER BACK — BACK LINE
LEFT BACK

PLAYERS' ROTATION

POSITIONS

Volleyball teams score by hitting the ball over the net, within the boundaries, so that the opposition is unable to return it. The team serving gains one point for doing this and continues serving. If the receiving team does it, it wins the right to serve. A game is 15 points, but it must be won by two points, thus a 14-14 tie continues until either team gains a two-point advantage.

When the serve changes hands, players rotate clockwise, so that each player gets to serve.

Three players may touch the ball before it goes over the net, so back line players *set-up* front line players with soft lobs so they can slam it downward, called *spiking*, or *killing*.

VOLLEYBALL COURT

7'11⅝" (MEN)
7'4⅛" (WOMEN)
ATTACK AREA/FRONTCOURT
ATTACK LINE/REAR SPIKER'S LINE
FRONT LINE
BACK LINE
29'6"
CENTER LINE
59"
10"
SIDELINE
END LINE
9'10" SERVING AREA

NET ANTENNA
STRETCHER STRING
TOP CABLE
NET SIDELINE MARKER
HEADBAND
NET 3'3"
BOTTOM NET CABLE
MESH/NET BODY
UPRIGHT
RATCHET/LIFT HANDLE
FLOOR PLATE

NET

Water polo is played by two seven-player teams. The object is to throw the ball into the opponent's goal while preventing the opposition from scoring. The team scoring the most goals wins. A game is played in four seven-minute *periods* in a pool at least 5'11" deep. Only the goalie may touch bottom. A team has 35 seconds to shoot or it loses the ball.

The ball is advanced by striking it, passing or swimming with it. Only the goalie may touch the ball with both hands simultaneously.

Ordinary fouls, like *splashing* or *pushing,* are penalized by loss of possession. *Major fouls,* such as *kicking, clubbing* and *submerging,* may result in a 45-second ejection or a penalty shot.

FIELD OF PLAY/POOL/BATH

SUBSTITUTES
FIELD PLAYERS
22 YDS.
9'10¼"
END OF FIELD OF PLAY
GOAL LINE
4-METERS LINE (13')
OFFSIDE LINE/2-METERS LINE (6'6")
33 YDS.
GOAL/CAGE
FLOATING PLATFORM
GOAL POST
NET
GOALIE
OUT OF BOUNDS
BOUNDARY ROPE
HALF-DISTANCE LINE
SIGNAL FLAG
REFEREE

EQUIPMENT

BALL
28" CIR.
WT: 15 OZ.
WHITE CAP
DARK BLUE CAP
PLAYER NUMBER
CHIN STRAP/ TAPE
EAR PROTECTOR

SHOT ON GOAL

GOALKEEPER/GOALIE
GOALIE'S RED CAP
TWO-METER MAN/ HOLE MAN/SETTER
DEFENSIVE FIELD PLAYERS

Water skiers compete in *slalom*, *jumping* and figure, or *trick skiing*, events.

Slalom requires a skier on one ski to swing around a course of six buoys. The speed of the tow boat increases on each run until it

reaches 36 mph; then the tow line is progressively shortened. The winner is the skier who completes the most runs without missing a buoy.

Jumping is judged on distance. Boats are limited to 35 mph, but skiers often attain speeds of 55 mph

at the *takeoff point*.

Trick skiers make two passes of 20 seconds each on a 200-yard course, during which they perform as many maneuvers as possible. They are judged on form and the difficulty of their tricks.

Lifters compete in ten categories grouped by body weight. Once a barbell is *loaded*, or ready, a lifter has two minutes to begin. Timing stops when the barbell is raised above the knees. Competition consists of snatch and clean-and-jerk, with final placement determined by combined weight in both lifts. Each *lifter* pre-selects weights he will attempt to lift. He has three chances to perform a '*good lift*.' Two of the *referees* must approve a lift, signaling 'good lift' with a white light and 'no lift' with a red light. Discs are color-coded by weight for spectators' benefit.

The sequence at top and right is of the two-hand snatch. The bottom sequence shows the two-hand clean-and-jerk, which is performed last.

LIFT-OFF PHASE

LIFT-OFF PHASE

SHIFT PHASE

POWER POSITION/JUMP POSITION

PULLING UNDER PHASE/DROPPING UNDER PHASE

SQUAT SNATCH/LOCKED-OUT POSITION

RECOVERY PHASE

RECOVERY PHASE

RECOVERY PHASE

SHIFT AND POWER PHASE

PULLING-UNDER PHASE

SQUAT CLEAN/
RECEIVING PHASE

DIP

JERK

AFTER RECEIVING JUDGES
'DOWN' SIGNAL

COMPLETED/COMPLETION

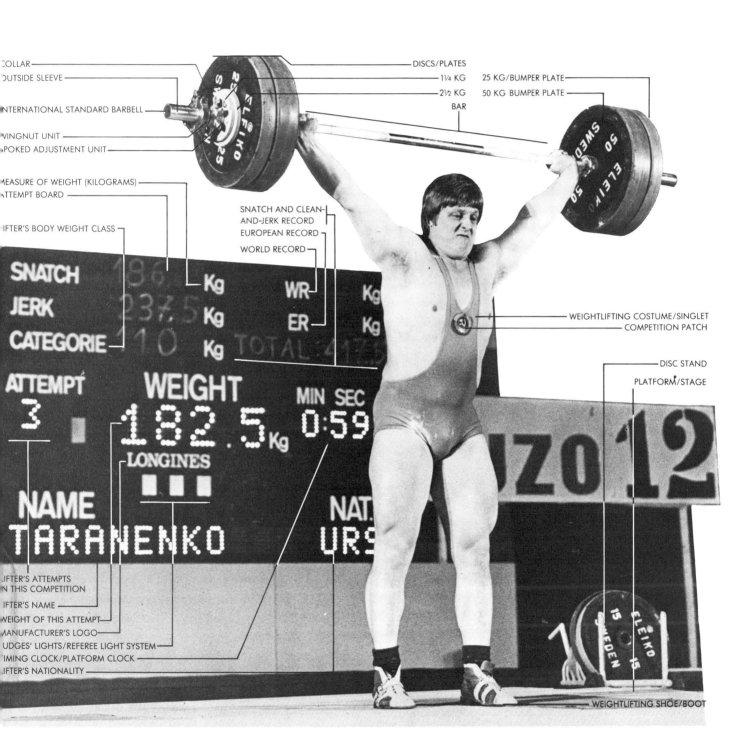

COLLAR

OUTSIDE SLEEVE

INTERNATIONAL STANDARD BARBELL

WINGNUT UNIT

SPOKED ADJUSTMENT UNIT

MEASURE OF WEIGHT (KILOGRAMS)

ATTEMPT BOARD

LIFTER'S BODY WEIGHT CLASS

DISCS/PLATES

1¼ KG

2½ KG

BAR

25 KG/BUMPER PLATE

50 KG BUMPER PLATE

SNATCH AND CLEAN-
AND-JERK RECORD

EUROPEAN RECORD

WORLD RECORD

WEIGHTLIFTING COSTUME/SINGLET

COMPETITION PATCH

DISC STAND

PLATFORM/STAGE

LIFTER'S ATTEMPTS
IN THIS COMPETITION

LIFTER'S NAME

WEIGHT OF THIS ATTEMPT

MANUFACTURER'S LOGO

JUDGES' LIGHTS/REFEREE LIGHT SYSTEM

TIMING CLOCK/PLATFORM CLOCK

LIFTER'S NATIONALITY

WEIGHTLIFTING SHOE/BOOT

If a *wrestler* holds his opponent's shoulders to the *mat* for a designated *count*, it is a *pin* or *fall*, and ends the *match* or *bout*. Otherwise, a match lasts three *periods* and is decided by a *point system*. A *referee* awards two points for a *takedown* (a wrestler taking his opponent to the mat and gaining *control*), a point for an *escape* (gaining *neutral position* from an opponent's control), two points for a *reversal* of control, and two or three points for a *near fall* or *near pin* (three when held for five seconds). A wrestler may be penalized one or two points, or disqualified for violations. A point is awarded for *riding time* if a wrestler has been in control a minute more than his opponent.

NEUTRAL POSITION/ STANDING POSITION

EARGUARD/HEADGUARD

WRESTLING SHORTS/UNIFORM/COSTUME

WRESTLING TIGHTS/UNIFORM/COSTUME

WRESTLING MAT

WRESTLING BOOTS/SHOES
TOURNAMENT COLOR TAPE
SCHOOL INITIAL
CENTER CIRCLE/CONTEST AREA/BOUNDARY

REFEREE'S POSITION/ NEW PERIOD STARTING POSITION

'OFFENSIVE' WRESTLER

'DEFENSIVE' WRESTLER

TAKEDOWN FROM NEUTRAL POSITION—TWO POINTS

TAKEDOWN AFTER NEUTRAL POSITION—HIP THROW

TIE UP FROM STANDING POSITION

TIE UP FROM KNEELING POSITION

Matches begin from a neutral position and wrestlers use *holds* and *counterholds*, which are set up by *feints*, *fakes*, *pushes* and *pulls* to gain advantage or control.

A takedown forces an opponent to support himself on his hands and knees. A *breakdown* flattens these supporting points until he is unable to free himself, or *escape*. 'Greco-Roman' wrestlers use only their legs for support and balance. In *free-style*, or *catch-as-catch-can*, wrestlers may use a variety of holds and *trips*. Japanese *sumo wrestling* matches end when one huge wrestler drives his equally huge opponent out of a 15' diameter ring or throws him to the ground.

PREDICAMENT OR NEAR FALL—TWO POINTS

NEAR FALL, ONE SHOULDER TO MAT—THREE POINTS

NEAR FALL, DEFENSIVE WRESTLER BRIDGE POSITION

REVERSAL OF ADVANTAGE POSITION OR SWITCH—TWO POINTS

PINNING POSITION—3/4 NELSON

PINNING POSITION—WINGS/FIGURE FOUR ON HEAD

PINNING POSITION—CRADLE

Sailboats, ranging in size from small, one-man *dinghies* to crewed *offshore racers*, compete over distances varying from short '*around the buoys*' courses to global circumnavigations. The standard Olympic course is a combination of triangles and *windward/leeward legs*, which are sailed zig-zag into the wind or off it.

In *one-design racing*, all boats in a *class* are identical, as in Olympic events. In *handicap racing*, dissimilar boats are assigned mathematically calculated time allowances. *Formula class racing* boats differ in appearance but comply to a formula which includes variables such as length, girth and sail area, and results in a number usually expressed in meters.

CREW

FOREDECK CREW
BOW MAN
MAST MAN
GRINDER
SAIL TRIMMER
AFTERGUARD | HELMSMAN
TACTICIAN

AMERICA'S CUP 1983 FINAL
DOWNWIND TACKING DUEL

AUSTRALIA II

WINDWARD MARK

LIBERTY

LIBERTY
JIBES

WIND

AUSTRALIA II
JIBES

AUSTRALIA II
BEARS OFF & PULLS AHEAD

OLYMPIC COURSE

WIND DIRECTION
COMMITTEE BOAT
WINDWARD MARK
FINISH LINE
FIRST LEG
SECOND LEG
THIRD LEG
FOURTH LEG
FIFTH LEG
SIXTH/FINAL LEG
LEEWARD MARK
STARTING LINE

Each yacht has its own sail plan—one or more sails designed for sailing at different angles to the wind and under different conditions.

The most common rig consists of a mainsail, or *main*, and a *headsail*. Most headsails are used when the boat is *going to windward*, sailing into the wind at about a 45 degree angle. These sails vary in size, from small *storm jibs*, used in heavy wind, to larger *working jibs*, used in moderate weather, to big genoas, set to catch lesser winds.

A spinnaker is used when sailing *downwind*, with the wind behind the boat, pushing it. Sail materials range from light *dacron* and *nylon* to heavy *kevlar*.

SPINNAKER RUN

MAINSAIL

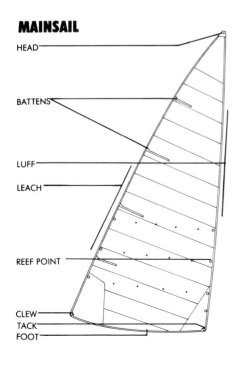

HEAD

BATTENS

LUFF

LEACH

REEF POINT

CLEW
TACK
FOOT

JIB/GENOA

HEAD

LEACH
LUFF

FOOT

SPINNAKER/TRI-RADIAL

HEAD

LEACH/LUFF

Olympic sailing classes range from sailboards, the smallest at 12 feet, to *catamaran* and *centerboard boats*, to *keel designs*, the largest at 26¾ feet.

Course flags on the committee boat signal the order in which spe-cific *buoys* or markers are to be rounded. At the start, *skippers* maneuver to cross the starting line when the starting gun or *hooter* sounds. The first boat to cross the finish line wins. In Olympic scoring, the yacht receiving the fewest points in a race series wins. First place finishers get 0 points, second get 3, and so on.

The Windglider, the sailboard used in the Olympics, is basically a surfboard with a sail sleeved on a rotating mast.

SAILBOARD

SAIL

MAST

WINDOW

BOARD

UNIVERSAL JOINT

BOOM/WISHBONE

SAILING HARNESS

DAGGERBOARD

SKEG

FOOT STRAPS

RACE START

SIGNAL FLAGS/
COURSE FLAGS

STARTING LINE

RACE COMMITTEE BOAT

MARK

MAST/SPAR/STICK

SHROUDS

HEADSTAY

BOOM

BOW

COCKPIT

MAINSHEET

FORWARD

TILLER

STARBOARD

PORT

STARBOARD QUARTER

AMIDSHIPS

KEEL

AFT

STERN

RUDDER
PORT QUARTER

BALL & SOCKET STEPPED MAST

MAST ROTATION CONTROL
MAINSAIL

MAINSAIL CLEW OUTHAUL
BATTEN/FULL LENGTH BATTEN
MAINSAIL LUFF DOWNHAUL

JIB HEADSTAY
TURNBUCKLE

HULLS

DIAMOND LINE

JIB HALYARD TENSION

REFERENCE MARKS FOR CLEW OUTHAUL POSITION
RED LINE CLEW OUTHAUL

COMPASS
BARBER MARKER

JIB BRIDLE

STARBOARD JIB SHEET

TRAPEZE HANDLE/ GRIP

MAINSHEET BLOCK

TRAPEZE SECURING WIRE
SHROUD

FORE/AFT JIB LEAD ADJUSTMENT

FORWARD/MAIN CROSSBEAM

TRAMPOLINE
MAINSHEET
LACING

SHROUD LENGTH ADJUSTER

TILLER

CENTERBOARD LINE

ATHWARTSHIP JIB LEAD ADJUSTMENT

RATCHET BLOCK

TELESCOPING TILLER EXTENSION

CENTERBOARD/CENTER PLATE

TRAVELER CONTROL
TILLER CROSSARM
PORT JIB SHEET
HIKING STRAP
MAINSHEET TRAVELER/HORSE

AFT CROSSBEAM

INSPECTION PORT

RUDDER STOCK

RUDDER-DOWN LINE

RUDDER

Powerboat racing is conducted on inland waters and offshore, in inboard or outboard motorboats or in inboard or outboard hydroplanes.

In offshore racing, boats in five classes compete at speeds of upwards of 170-mph over courses that vary in length from 80 to 160 miles. Boats range in size, from 17 to 50 feet in length; in power, ranging from 400-hp to 2,500-hp multi-engine configurations; and in design, either *catamaran hulls*, which are faster on smooth water, or *V-shaped* *monohulls*, which withstand heavy seas better.

Unlimited hydroplanes, or *thunderboats*, compete in their own race circuit.

OFFSHORE CREW

UNLIMITED HYDROPLANE

COMMAND CONSOLE

Non-racing powerboats are used to fish or dive from, or for *cruising* different *ports o'call* or stopping at various *anchorages*, called *gunkholing*.

Motorboats also engage in *rendezvous*, in which several powerboats congregate in one location for a series of events, including seminars on nautical subjects, and *predicted log contests*, in which skippers, relying on compass, engine tachometers and *charts* alone, power their boats over a course, passing prearranged *checkpoints* at exact times predicted before the start of the race. Errors, either fast or slow, are totaled by an on-board observer using a *timepiece*. The skipper with the smallest error wins.

DECK

COMPANIONWAY DOOR
UPPER HELM STATION
WINDSHIELD
FLYING BRIDGE
HANDRAIL
ANCHOR RODE
FLYBRIDGE LADDER
HANDRAIL
CLEAT
HATCH
PORTLIGHT
TOERAIL
SALOON DOOR
SALOON WINDOW

HULL

GALLEY
ROPE & CHAIN LOCKER
HEAD
SHOWER/STALL SHOWER
TOILET/MSD/MARINE SANITATION DEVICE
SINK
MASTER STATEROOM
FORWARD V-BERTHS
LOWER HELM STATION
DINING TABLE
SETTEE
QUEEN-SIZED BERTH
ENGINE ROOM
SWIM LADDER
SWIM PLATFORM
ENGINE
RUDDER
HANGING LOCKER/STORAGE
SHAFT
STRUT
PROPELLER/PROP/SCREW
ZINK

The *sportsfisherman, sportfisherman, sportfisher,* or *sportfish* shown here is distinguished by a large *cockpit,* used to facilitate fighting *gamefish,* and is normally operated by a *captain* and *mate* who often double as wireman and gaffman.

The tower control is used to position *baits* and spot *strikes*. The lower station is used when the fish is alongside the boat, prior to *boating, tagging* or *releasing* it. The flybridge controls are used when the boat is en route to the *fishing grounds*.

WIND DIRECTION INDICATOR

TOWER CONTROLS

ENGINE CLUTCHES

WHEEL

ENGINE THROTTLES

FISH-CAUGHT FLAG
TOWER PLATFORM/TOWER DECK
TOWER STANCHION
FLAG HALYARD
RADAR ANTENNA
VENTURI WINDSHIELD
DANFORTH ANCHOR
CHOCK/FAIRLEAD

PULPIT

BOWSPRIT

PLOW ANCHOR

WINDLASS

HATCH

FOREDECK

BOW RAIL

STANCHION

PORTS

FLYING BRIDGE

SIDE DECK

SHEER LINE

ENGINE AIR INTAKE
CLEAT
BAIT BOX/FREEZER
RUB RAIL
COCKPIT
ROD HOLDER
DOCK LINE HAWSEPIPE
TRANSOM DOOR/GATE
STERN LIGHT
SWIM PLATFORM

-DAVIS-

—AUTOMATIC DIRECTION FINDING ANTENNA

LORAN AND RADIO ANTENNAS

TOWER BIMINI

OUTRIGGERS

ANEMOMETER

TOWER/TUNA TOWER

LADDER

FLYBRIDGE BIMINI

SPREADERS

FATHOMETER

CHIEF OPERATING STATION/CONTROL CONSOLE

NAVIGATOR'S SEAT

HELMSMAN'S CHAIR/HELMSEAT

GAFF

SLIDING DOOR

LOWER CONTROL STATION/COCKPIT CONTROL STATION

ROD

TACKLE CABINET

GUNWALE

COAMING

GIMBALED ROD HOLDER

FOOTREST

FIGHTING CHAIR/ BARBER CHAIR

BOARDING LADDER

COCKPIT CREW

WIREMAN

GAFFMAN

ANGLER/'THE CRANK'

TRANSOM

FIGHTING CHAIR

CONTROL CONSOLE

FUEL GAUGE

ENGINE HOUR METER

ENGINE OIL-PRESSURE GAUGE

WATER TEMPERATURE GAUGE

GEAR OIL-PRESSURE GAUGE

VOLTMETER

PORT-ENGINE CLUTCH

COMPASS

TACHOMETERS

BILGE AND FUEL ALARMS

PORT THROTTLE

STARBOARD-ENGINE CLUTCH

WHEEL

ENGINE STOP

TRIM TABS

STARBOARD THROTTLE

Cruising sailboats are designed to accommodate skipper and crew on *offshore passages* and on *coastal cruises*, called *coasting*. Although most yachts over 20 feet in length are equipped with mechanical propulsion, called *auxiliary power*, crews rely on a selection of sails cut to particular specifications for different wind conditions.

A sailboat moving before, or in front of, the wind is said to be *running*; when moving across the wind it is *reaching*; when sailing into the wind it is *tacking*.

Shifting sails from one side of the boat to the other is called a *tack* when sailing into the wind, a *jibe* when sailing off the wind.

DECK

HULL

COMMISSIONER'S TROPHY—
BASEBALL

STANLEY CUP—
HOCKEY

OLYMPIC MEDAL

LOMBARDI TROPHY—
PRO FOOTBALL

DAVIS CUP—
TENNIS

O'BRIEN TROPHY—
PRO BASKETBALL

**U.S. OPEN TROPHY—
GOLF**

**AMERICA'S CUP—
YACHTING**

**INDIANAPOLIS 500 TROPHY—
AUTO RACING**

**CHAMPIONSHIP BELT—
BOXING**

INDEX

front thwart, canoe 44
front wall, court handball 99
front wall, racquetball court 136
front wall, squash racquets court 160
front wheel, dragster 21
front wheel quick release, road racing bicycle 51
front wing/air foil/spoiler, dragster 21
front wing/spoiler/dive plane, race car 17
frontis/front wall, jai alai cancha 113
fronton, jai alai 112
fuel filler, sports car 22
fuel gauge, competition fishing boat 207
fuel gauge, motorcycle 130
fuel hose, automobile racing pit 19
fuel hoses, ballooning basket 5
fuel intake valve, race car 17
fuel line, ballooning basket 5
fuel overflow hose, automobile racing pit 19
fuel overflow man, automobile racing pit crew 19
fuel tank, ballooning basket 5
fuel tank, dragster 21
fuel tank, Formula One aircraft cockpit (air racing) 4
fuel tank, kart 114
fuel tank, motocross bike 129
fuel tank, motorcycle 130
fuel tank lock, motorcycle 130
fuel tank straps, ballooning basket 5
fuel valve, race car 17
full-pipe event, skateboarding 149
full-posing routine, bodybuilding 37
full wind-up, pitching (baseball) 28
fullbacks, Gaelic football 81
fullbacks, hurling 106
fullbacks, soccer formations 156
fullface helmet, automobile racing pit crew 19
funny cars, drag racing 20
fuselage, Formula One aircraft (air racing) 4
fuselage, race car 17
fuselage/hull, iceboat 107

'G' meter, Formula One aircraft cockpit (air racing) 4
'G' meter, glider cockpit (aerial sports) 6
Gaelic football/football/ball 81
Gaelic football 81
gaff, angling 14
gaff, competition fishing boat 207
gaff, deep sea fishing 15
gaffman, competition fishing boat 206, 207
gainer/Mohlberg, diving 57
gaits, harness horses 104
galley, cruising sailboat (yachting) 208
galley, motoryacht hull 205
game, bowling 38
game, football 75
game, tennis 169
game birds, skeet shooting 147
game fish/fish 9
game number, jai alai scoreboard/betting board 112
gamefish 8, 206
gap, fishhook 9
gap/daylight, football 77
gas pedal/throttle kart 114
gastrocnemius muscle, bodybuilder 36
gate, cruising sailboat (yachting) 208
gate, horse-racing 101

gate, slalom kayaking 46
gate bar/bar, hurdle (track and field) 176
gate judges, whitewater slalom (canoeing & kayaking) 46
gate number, (flat) horse-racing 101
gate/transom door, competition fishing boat 206
gate/upright, equestrian show jumping fence 62
gate upright, hurdle (track and field) 176
gauntlet/handguard/kote, kendo (martial arts) 128
gear housing, spinning reel (angling) 12
gear oil-pressure gauge, competition fishing boat 207
gear/tackle/fishing equipment, tackle box 9
genoa/jib, yachting 200
get-ready position/neutral position, table tennis 166
giant, rings trick (gymnastics) 94
giant slalom Alpine skiing 150
giant swing grip change, horizontal bar (gymnastics) 95
gill cover/operculum/opercule preopercle, fish 9
gill opening, fish 9
gimbal, big game rod (angling) 15
gimbaled rod holder, competition fishing boat 207
gimbals, fighting chair (angling) 15
girdle pad/hip pad, football equipment 79
girth, harness horse racing 103
girth & surcingle, polo pony 134
girth & surcingle, racehorse 102
girth pad, racehorse 102
gladiator, boxing slang 42
glass, basketball backboard 30
glass, court handball 99
glass, ice hockey rink 108
glass jaw/china chin/cement chin, boxing slang 42
glassless window, stock car 22
glide, shot putting technique (track and field) 181
glide, swimming 164
glide kip, uneven parallel bars (gymnastics) 97
glide/runner, shuffleboard cue 148
glider, aerial sports 6
glider cockpit, aerial sports 6
glove, fencing 65
glove, field hockey goalie 69
glove, jai alai 113
glove, lacrosse 115, 116
glove, luge 118
glove, scuba diver (diving/spear fishing) 58
glove, ski jumper 153
glove, skier 150
glove, soccer goalie 155
glove/gloved hand/handhold, rodeo bareback bronc riding 137
glove/mitt, baseball 26
glove model, baseball glove 26
glove racquetball 136
glove studs, luge 118
gloves, bobsledder 34
gloves, ice hockey 110
gloves, riding (equestrian events) 63
GO-light, on drag racing Christmas tree 20, 21

go position, sprints (track and field) 174
goal, field hockey 68, 69
goal, Gaelic football 81
goal, hurling 106
goal, ice hockey 108
goal, lacrosse 116
goal, roller hockey rink 140
goal, rugby field 143
goal, rugby 143
goal, soccer field 156
goal, soccer 155
goal, team handball 100
goal area, lacrosse field 115
goal area, soccer field 156
goal area/circle, team handball 100
goal area line, team handball 100
goal/cage, water polo 192
goal crease, ice hockey rink 108
goal/goalpost/uprights, football 75
goal/head/house, curling 50
goal judge box, ice hockey rink 108
goal/hoop/basket, basketball 30
goal kick, soccer 156
goal line, field hockey 68, 69
goal line, ice hockey rink 108,109
goal line, polo ground 134
goal line, soccer field 156
goal line, team handball 100
goal line, water polo 192
goal-line defensive team, football 76
goal line/try line, rugby field 143
goal net, ice hockey rink 108
goal pad, ice hockey goalkeeper 110
goal post, field hockey 69
goal post, ice hockey goalie 110
goal post, polo ground 134
goal post, water polo field 192
goal post/upright, soccer 155
goal posts, rugby 143
goal tending, basketball officials' signal 32
goalie, roller hockey rink 140
goalie, water polo field 192
goalie equipment, field hockey 69
goalie glove, soccer 155
goalie/goaltender, lacrosse field 115
goalie stick, ice hockey 110
goalie's red cap, water polo field 192
goalkeeper/goalie, field hockey pitch 68
goalkeeper/goalie/goaler, ice hockey 110
goalkeeper/goalie, water polo goal 192
goalkeeper/goalie, soccer 155
goalkeeper/goalie, team handball 100
goalkeeper, soccer formations 156
goalkeeper's penalty line, roller hockey rink 140
goalpost, hurling net 106
goaltender, Gaelic football 81
goaltenders, hurling 106
goggles, bobsledder 34
goggles, court handball 99
goggles, iceboating 107
goggles, jockey (horse racing) 102
goggles, motocross rider 131
goggles, racquetball 136
goggles, ski jumper 153
goggles, skier 150
goggles, swimming 163
gold/bullseye/10, archery target 16
golf bag & club set 84
golf ball 84

golf cart/caddy cart 84
golf cart path, golf course 82
golf club/wood 82
golf clubs 84, 85
golf course/links 82
golf green 82
golf shoes 84
golf swing 83
golf tee 82, 84
golf 82–86
golfer 82
gondola/basket, ballooning 5
good lift, weightlifting 194
'goofy foots,' surfing 161
gooseneck, cruising sailboat (yachting) 208
gooseneck, iceboat 107
gooseneck/main standard, football goal 75
gore seams, ballooning 5
grace, bodybuilding 36
grace, figure skating 71
Grand Touring (GT), sports car racing 22
grandstand, baseball field 25
grandstand and clubhouse area horse-racing track 101
grandstands, automobile racetrack 18
grandstands, cycling velodrome 52
grass court, bocce 35
gravity waves, swimming 163
Greco-Roman wrestling 198
green/bowling green, lawn bowling 117
green flag, automobile racing 17
green (timed period has begun), on field event timer (track and field) 189
greyhound performance rating (dog racing) 59
greyhound racing 59
gridiron/football field 76
grinder, yacht-racing crew 199
grip, Alpine ski pole 150
grip, badminton racket 23
grip, big game rod (angling) 15
grip, canoe paddle 44
grip, golf clubs 85
grip, hammer (track and field) 183
grip, hurling hurley 106
grip, softball bat 158
grip, spear gun (spear fishing) 58
grip ball, pitcher's set position (baseball) 28
grip/handguard/palm protector, horizontal bar (gymnastics) 95
grip/handle, croquet mallet 49
grip/handle, racquetball racquet 136
grip/handle, squash racket 160
grip/handle, tennis racket 169
grip safety, target pistol 145
grip tape, skateboard 149
grip/trapeze handle, yachting 203
grips, table tennis 166
groin, boxing slang 42
groin, martial arts striking point 126
groin strap, fencer 65
grommets, fighting chair harness (angling) 15
grooming, bodybuilding 36
groove, automobile racing 17
'groove,' luge 118
grooves/tracking, ski jumping 153
ground cloth/pad/blanket, rifle shooting 144
ground strokes, tennis 171

tower bimini, competition fishing boat 207

tower controls, competition fishing boat 206

tower platform/tower deck, competition fishing boat 206

tower stanchion, competition fishing boat 206

tower/tuna tower, competition fishing boat 207

towline/ski rope, water skier 193

traces/tracing, figure skating 71

track, automobile racing 18, 20, 22

track, cycling velodrome 52

track, luge 118

track, rabbit (dog racing) 59

track, scull (rowing) 141

track, ski jumping 153

track, speed skating 159

track and field 173–189

track bike, cycling 52

track condition, past performance chart (horse racing) 103

track/course, dog racing 59

track/drag strip/dragway, drag racing 20

track meets, track and field 173

track secretary, horse racing 102

track shoes, scull (rowing) 141

track/skating surface, speed (roller) skating 140

track/trail, cross country skiing 154

tracking/grooves, ski jumping 153

trademark/label, baseball bat 26

traffic line/barrier/railing, speed (roller) skating 140

trail leg, high-jump straddle (track and field) 185

trail rope, ballooning 5

trailing leg, hurdling technique (track and field) 176

trailing leg, steeplechase (track and field) 177

trainer, dog racing 60

trainer, fighter's corner (boxing) 42

trainer, horse-racing program entry 103

trainer, past performance chart (horse racing) 103

trajectories, skeet and trapshooting ranges 147, 148

trampoline, yachting 203

transition curve, ski jumping 153

transitions, dressage (equestrian events) 63

transom, cruising sailboat (yachting) 208

transom door/gate, competition fishing boat 206

trap, trap and skeet shooting range 147

trap house/low house, skeet shooting range 147

trap number, dog racing 59

trap release/pulling mechanism, trapshooting 146

trap/skeet & trap machine, shooting 147

trap window, skeet shooting range 147

trapeze handle/grip, yachting 203

trapeze securing wire, yachting 203

trapezius muscle, bodybuilder 36

traphouse, trapshooting 146

trapping a soccer ball 157

trapshooting 146

trapshooting range, shooting 146

trapshooting range 146

travel set, angling 12

traveler control, yachting 203

traveling, basketball officials' signal 32

travels, gymnastics 93

treble hook, plug (angling) 12

tree/frame, polo saddle 134

trench shooting/trapshooting 146

trenches, football 77

tri-radial/spinnaker, yachting 200

triceps muscle, bodybuilder 36

trick skiing, water skiing 193

tricks, gymnastics 88

trifecta, bet (horse racing) 103

trigger, shotgun (skeet and trapshooting) 146

trigger, target pistol 145

trigger, water ski 193

trigger guard, shotgun (skeet and trapshooting) 146

trigger mechanisms, spear gun (spear fishing) 58

trigger stop, target pistol 145

trim, baseball pants 26

trim, fencing mask 65

trim, running shoe (track and field) 178

trim tabs, competition fishing boat 207

trim tape/binding, tennis racket 169

trip/dog, spinning reel (angling) 12

triple, baseball 25

triple bars/staircase, equestrian show jumping fence 62

triple bogey, golf 86

triple jump/hop, step and jump, track and field 184

triple jump takeoff, jumping area (track and field) 184

triple ring/triple-score ring, dart board 53

tripping, field hockey 69

tripping, football officials' signal 80

tripping, ice hockey officials' signal 111

tripping, soccer foul 157

trips, wrestling 198

trolling, angling 13

trolling motor, bass boat 13

trolling reel, angling 13

trophies 209

trot, dressage (equestrian events) 63

trotters, horse racing 104

trotting and pacing gaits, harness horse racing 104

trough, wave (surfing) 161

trousers, jai alai 113

trousers/knickers/pantaloons, fencer 65

truck, roller skate 140

truck, skateboard 149

truck bolt/king pin/action bolt, roller skate 140

true drive, golf 85

trunk, fish 9

trunk development/upper body development, bodybuilder 37

trunks, boxer 41

trunks, speed (roller) skating 140

trunks/shorts/pants, lacrosse 116

try, rugby 143

try line/goal line, rugby field 143

tube, skate 159

tube lure, umbrella rig (angling) 13

tube/pipeline, wave (surfing) 161

'tubing,' surfing 161

tuck, synchronized swimming position 162

tuck position, diving 56

tuck position, parallel bars routine (gymnastics) 96

tug, gliding (aerial sports) 6

tumbling, gymnastics 88, 89

tumbling movement/cartwheel, balance beam (gymnastics) 98

tunnel, track and field 173

tunnel entrance, cycling velodrome 52

turbocharger, race car 17

turbocharger popoff valve, race car 17

turbocharger wastegate, race car 17

turf, baseball slang 25

turf course & steeplechase course, horse-racing track 101

turf/field, polo 134

turn, shot putting technique (track and field) 181

turn, swimming 163

turn, track and field 173

turn and slip indicator, glider cockpit (aerial sports) 6

turn/pivot/spin/rotation, discus throwing technique (track and field) 182

turn signal, motorcycle 130

turnbuckle, boxing ring 41

turnbuckle, cruising sailboat (yachting) 208

turnbuckle, yachting 203

turning buoys, kayaking racecourse 45

turning buoys, slalom course (water skiing) 193

turning light, motorcycle 130

turnout, horse and rider in dressage (equestrian events) 63

turns, freestyle figure skating 72, 73

twenty-four-second clock/shot clock, basketball 30

twenty-point must system, amateur boxing 42

twist, tennis serve 170

twist dive 57

two-finger spear hand, martial arts fighting 127

two-hand snatch/snatch, weightlifting 194, 195

two-hundred-meter, heptathlon (track and field) 188

two-meter man/hole man/setter, shot on water polo goal 192

two pin, bowling 39

two-point conversion, football 78

two-way swivel, surf fishing rigs 14

Uke, aikido (martial arts) 124

umbrella, golf bag & club set 84

umbrella rig, angling 13

umpire, baseball 29

umpire, cricket ground & pitch 48

umpire, football officials 80

umpire/chair umpire, tennis–center court 168

umpire signals, cricket 48

umpires, polo 134, 135

umpires/judges, tennis–center court 168

unanimous decision, boxing match 41

unavoidable hinders, racquetball 136

unbalancing zone/pre-attack zone 168

underarm protector, fencing equipment 65

undercut/cut, pommel horse routine (gymnastics) 93

underserve line/fault line, jai alai cancha 113

undershirt, baseball 26

underwater hockey, breathhold diving game 58

unemployed leg/free leg, figure skating 71

uneven parallel bars/asymmetrical bars, gymnastics 97

unfair tackle from behind, soccer officials' signal 157

uniform (see also costume, suit)

uniform, automobile racing pit crew 19

uniform, football 79

uniform, Gaelic football 81

uniform, wrestling 196

uniform jersey, football uniform 79

uniform shirt/blouse, baseball player 26

uniforms, baseball 26

universal joint, sailboard (yachting) 201

unlimited-class races, motorcycling 130

unlimited hydroplane, powerboat racing (yachting) 204

unsportsmanlike conduct, ice hockey officials' signal 111

upfield, football 77

upper back, martial arts striking point 126

upper body development, bodybuilder 37

upper deck, automobile racetrack 18

upper helm station, motoryacht deck 205

upper jaw, fish 9

upper limb, archery bow 16

upper panel, ice hockey skate 108

upper stitching, curling broom 50

upper wing, biplane (aerial sports–aerobatics) 2

uppercut, boxing punch 43

uppers, running shoe (track and field) 178

upright, croquet wicket 49

upright, football goal 75

upright, horizontal bar (gymnastics) 95

upright, parallel bars (gymnastics) 96

upright, steeplechase dry hurdle (track and field) 177

upright, vaulting horse (gymnastics) 92

upright, volleyball net 191

upright/column/stanchion, basketball 30

upright/goal post, soccer 155

upright handlebars, track racing bicycle 52

upright position, balance beam (gymnastics) 98

upright position, sprints (track and field) 174

upright/standard, high-jumping area (track and field) 185

upright/standard, pole vault (track and field) 186

uprights, equestrian show jumping fences 62

uprights/goal/goalposts, football 75

upshot, archery 16

upstairs/attic/belfry, boxing slang 42

upstream gate, whitewater slalom (canoeing & kayaking) 46

upward thrust/upsweep, relays baton handoff (track and field) 175

using a fighting chair, angling 15

V-shaped monohulls, powerboat racing (yachting) 204

ACKNOWLEDGEMENTS

1–2, Christen Industries, Inc.; 5, Raven Industries; 9, Oberlin Canteen Company, Wisconsin Division of Tourism; 11, Orvis Company, Martin Reel Company, Don Zahner, A.J. McClaine; 12, Martin Reel Company; 13, Shakespeare Company, S&K Products, Inc.; 15, Murray Brothers, Rosemary Murray; 16, National Archery Association, Easton Aluminum, Inc., Kathy O'Brien; 17, Deke Holgate Enterprises, Penzoil Products Company; 18–19, Indianapolis Motor Speedway; 20–21, Les Lovett, National Hot Rod Association, Deke Houlgate Enterprises, Ron McQueen; 22, Wayne Baker; 23, U.S. Badminton Association, Carlton Corporation; 26, Rawlings, Adirondack; 27, Tony Ferrara; 34, Tip Sempliner, Chelsea Designs; 35, International Bocce Association; 36–37, Kerri Keenan; 38, Brunswick Corporation, Murray Lanes; 40–43, Caesars Palace, Tuf-Wear Company, U.S.A. Amateur Boxing Federation, Madison Square Garden; 50, Air Canada; 53, Sportcraft, Larry Gazley, The Dart Store; 58, The A.B. Biller Company; 59–60, American Greyhound Track Association; 63-64, American Horse Shows Association; 68, Sportcraft, India Press Information Bureau; 75, 79, James Ramey; New York Jets; 82, Professional Golfer's Association, Kathy Gallagher; 84, Champion, Colombia, Titalist; 86, Professional Golfer's Association; 88, Brenda Bernhardt Frasca, Manhattan Gymnastic Center, NYC; 90, A.B. Fredericks; 91–95, Nissen; 98, Fuji Film, Dave Black; 99, U.S. Handball Association, Saranac Gloves; 100, Peter Bruehning, U.S. Handball Team Association; 101, Churchill Downs, Ruidoso Downs; 102, Meadowlands Racetrack, Ruidoso Sunland, Dick Alwan; 104, Meadowlands Racetrack; 105, Sportcraft; 106, Irish Press; 112, Dania Jai Alai; 113, Milford Jai Alai; 114, International Kart Federation, Doug Stokes, Cartman Company; 115, STX Company; 117, Henselite Company, Australian Tourist Bureau; 119–128, World Taekwondo Academy, Loren Lalli, Japan National Tourist Organization, Japan Air Lines, Noburu Kataoka, Linda Sakariasen, John Antonellis, Vincent De Martino, Bobby Troka, Harlan Cary Poe, Andy Nichols; 129–130, Kawasaki; 132, Silva Company, Johnson Camping, Precise International, U.S. Orienteering Federation, Al Smith; 133, U.S. Platform Tennis Association, Jim McNerney, ACE; 134, Polo Magazine, Saddle Shop, Fifth Avenue Polo Imports; 136, Sportcraft; 138, International Professional Rodeo Association; 139–140, U.S. Amateur Confederation of Roller Skating; 148, Susan Koenig; 153–154, Austrian Travel Bureau, Saranac; 155, Chicago Sting, Sgt. Frank Karcher; 158, U.S. Softball Association, Kathy Aronson, DeBeer; 160, AMF/Voit; 161, Surfing Magazine; 166–167, U.S. Table Tennis Association, Malcolm Anderson, Martin Kilpatrick, Table Tennis Company, Michigan Ladder Company; 168, British Tourist Authority; 171–172, Virginia Slims; 174, Cramer Moore; 178, Converse, Northwestern University; 180–181, Adidas; 182, AAF; 185, Adidas; 186, 188, Beth Goodman, Portapit; 189, AAE, Sportcraft, Cronus; 190, Mikasa, U.S. Olympic Volleyball Team; 191, Sports Imports; 192, Porter Equipment Company, U.S. Water Polo Incorporated, Gregory Kincheloe; 193, Connelly; 194–195, U.S. Weightlifting Federation, Harvey Newton; 196–198, Housatonic Valley Regional High School, Michael Thompson, Thomas Breuler; 204, Budweiser.

In addition, the editors would like to acknowledge the contributions of the staff at Hammond, Inc., without whom this book could not possibly have been done. These include, but are certainly not limited to Publisher Hugh Johnson, a friend in difficult times, copy editors extraordinaire Dorothy Bacheller and Sherry Wheaton Wert, and the Mark Resnick Express. We also appreciate the support of Richard Curtis, Richard Curtis Literary Agency.

PHOTO CREDITS

Page 4 Jim Vliet; 6 (bottom) George Uveges, Santa Monica, Calif.; 7 (top left, right) Cos Colgrove, (bottom left) M. Anderson Jenkins, Wittier, Calif.; 8 Burton McNeely; 17 (top) Ron McQueeney; 18 John Gray, Indianapolis Motor Speedway; 19 (top) Ron McQueeney, (bottom) Tom Lucas; 20 Les Lovett; 22 (top) Sheila Hill, (bottom) Rusty Jarett; 23 (bottom) Martin Hoke; 24 Joe DiMaggio, Centerport, NY; 25 (bottom) Al Messerschmidt, Miami Beach, Fla.; 27 (sequential) Globus Brothers/Steve Borowski, New York City, NY, (middle) Betty Suyker, NYC, NY, (bottom) Al Messerschmidt; 28–29 Globus Brothers/Steve Borowski, NYC, NY; 30 (bottom right) Brent Nicastro, Madison, Wis.; 31 (left) Betty Suyker, (right) © Estate of Ben Rose/Courtesy Sol Shamilzadeh, New York City, NY, (bottom right) Brent Nicastro; 32 (left) Brent Nicastro, (right) Betty Suyker; 34 Nancie Battaglia, Lake Placid, New York; 35 Dennis Floss; 36–37 Phillip Stark, New York City, NY; 40 Joe DiMaggio; 41 (top) Al Messerschmidt, (bottom) Bob Davis, Reno, Nevada; 42 (left) Ben Rose, (top right) Al Messerschmidt, (bottom right) Bob Davis; 45 Frank Dallas; 46 James Thresher; 49 (top right) Cliff Johnson, Loxahtchee, Fla.; 50 (lower right) Michael Burns; 51 Brent Nicastro; 52 (right) Robert George/Velo-News, Brattleboro, Vt., (left) Long Photography, Los Angeles, Calif.; 54 (bottom) Joe DiMaggio; 58 (lower right) Reg Bragonier; 62 David Fisher; 63 Bodo Hangan; 65 Globus Brothers/Steve Borowski; 66 (top) Jeff Bukantz, (bottom) Globus Brothers/Steve Borowski; 67 Globus Brothers/Steve Borowski; 69, 70 Eduardo Patino, New York City, NY; 74 Eduardo Patino; 78 Richard Dubin, Tampa, Fla.; 79 (top) David Fisher, (bottom) Richard Dubin; 83 Ben Rose; 87 Ben Rose; 88–89 Globus Brothers/Steve Borowski; 92 Roman Leos, Los Angeles, Calif.; 94 Roman Leos; 96 Roman Leos; 97 Ben Rose; 98 (top) Ben Rose, (bottom left) Roman Leos; 107 Sharon Green; 112 (top) Ben Rose; 114 Doug Stokes; 118 Nancie Battaglia; 119 Ben Rose; 120–121 Globus Brothers/Steve Borowski; 122 Phillip Stark; 123 (top right) Phillip Stark; 124-125 Phillip Stark; 128 (bottom) Globus Brothers/Steve Borowski; 129 (right) Guy Gurney, New York City, NY; 131 Guy Gurney; 132 (top) Al Smith, US Orienteering Federation; 135 (right) Al Messerschmidt; 137 Ginny Southworth, Aiken, South Carolina; 138 (top left) Brent Nicastro, (top center, top right) Ginny Southworth; 139 Ted Kirk; 142 (right) Joe DiMaggio; 143 Brent Nicastro; 145–148 Joe DiMaggio; 149 Bruce Walker, Melbourne, Fla.; 154 (bottom center, bottom right) Nancie Battaglia; 157 (top) Globus Brothers/Steve Borowski; 158 (top) Globus Brothers/Steve Borowski; 160 (right) Robert H. Lehman, New York City, NY; 161 Aaron Chang; 162 Nancy Hines, Santa Clara, Calif.; 163 (top three) Brent Nicastro; 165 (bottom left, top right) Brent Nicastro; 166–167 Malcolm Anderson; 169 (bottom right) Globus Brothers/Steve Borowski; 174 (top) Globus Brothers/Steve Borowski, (middle, right) Brent Nicastro; 177 Rich Clarkson, Denver, Colorado; 178–179 (top) Globus Brothers/Steve Borowski; 180 Al Messerschmidt; 181 Joe DiMaggio; 182 (top left) Joe DiMaggio; 183 Al Messerschmidt; 184 Joe DiMaggio; 186 (bottom) Rich Clarkson; 187 Rich Clarkson; 192 Bud Symes; 194–195 Bruce Klemens, Clifton, New Jersey; 196–198 John Thompson; 199 Guy Gurney; 200 Guy Gurney; 201 Guy Gurney; 204 (top left) Guy Gurney

AFTERWORD

WHAT'S WHAT™ books are designed to provide visual and verbal access to the physical world. At the conclusion of the first volume in this series we invited readers to correspond with us, letting us know where the book proved useful and suggesting improvements and corrections. We were extremely pleased to have received replies from around the world and have attempted to incorporate many of the suggestions into this book. To ensure that WHAT'S WHAT™ IN SPORTS, as well as future volumes in the WHAT'S WHAT™ series, continues to provide accurate information in an entertaining manner, we invite readers of this volume to write us. We would like to know how successfully this book fulfilled your needs and expectations. We would also like to know in what subject areas future volumes in the WHAT'S WHAT™ information series would be most helpful to you. Please correspond with us at:

David Fisher
Reginald Bragonier Jr.
WHAT'S WHAT™ BOOKS
357 West 19th Street
New York, New York
10019